NORDIC
KNITS

Brimming with creative inspiration, how-to projects, and useful information to enrich your everyday life, Quarto Knows is a favorite destination for those pursuing their interests and passions. Visit our site and dig deeper with our books into your area of interest: Quarto Creates, Quarto Cooks, Quarto Homes, Quarto Lives, Quarto Drives, Quarto Explores, Quarto Gifts, or Quarto Kids.

First Published in 2021 by Voyageur Press, an imprint of The Quarto Group,
100 Cummings Center, Suite 265-D, Beverly, MA 01915, USA.
T (978) 282-9590 F (978) 283-2742 QuartoKnows.com

Voyageur Press titles are also available at discount for retail, wholesale, promotional, and bulk purchase. For details, contact the Special Sales Manager by email at specialsales@quarto.com or by mail at The Quarto Group, Attn: Special Sales Manager, 100 Cummings Center, Suite 265-D, Beverly, MA 01915, USA.

25 24 23 22 21   1 2 3 4 5

ISBN: 978-0-7603-7355-2

Digital edition published in 2021
eISBN: 978-0-7603-7356-9

Library of Congress Cataloging-in-Publication Data

Names: Flanders, Sue, 1960- author. | Kosel, Janine, 1964- author. |
     Hélène Magnússon, 1969- author.
Title: Nordic knits : 42 beautiful patterns to knit and keep you cozy / Sue
     Flanders, Janine Kosel & Hélène Magnússon.
Description: Beverly, MA : Voyageur Press, 2022. | Includes index. |
     Summary: "Nordic Knits offers 50 authentic, Scandinavian-inspired
     patterns for hats, mittens, and gloves-including stylish, traditional
     projects from Sweden, Norway, and Iceland"-- Provided by publisher.
Identifiers: LCCN 2021045477 (print) | LCCN 2021045478 (ebook) | ISBN
     9780760373552 (trade paperback) | ISBN 9780760373569 (ebook)
Subjects: LCSH: Knitting--Sweden--Patterns. | Knitting--Norway--Patterns. |
     Knitting--Iceland--Patterns.
Classification: LCC TT819.S8 .F538 2022 (print) | LCC TT819.S8 (ebook) |
     DDC 746.43/204109481--dc23
LC record available at https://lccn.loc.gov/2021045477
LC ebook record available at https://lccn.loc.gov/2021045478

Design: Ashley Prine, Tandem Books
Cover Image: Arnaldur Halldórsson
Page Layout: Ashley Prine, Tandem Books
Schematics and Charts: Barbara Drewlo and Mandy Kimlinger
Additional Image Credits: yarn pattern © Savurovan/Shutterstock; yarn icon © AVIcon/Shutterstock

Printed in China

NORDIC
KNITS

44 Beautiful Patterns to Knit and Keep You Cozy

Sue Flanders, Janine Kosel
& Hélène Magnússon

VOYAGEUR PRESS

CONTENTS

INTRODUCTION

Nordic Knits is an exploration in knitwear inspired by the traditional knitting styles of Norway, Sweden, and Iceland. These three countries, steeped in textile history, offer a wealth of inspiration to draw on. The patterns throughout were influenced by the different cultures and practices native to each country.

Think of the Norwegian sweaters that we love so much (and need in cold climates)—they have very humble beginnings. Some of the earliest sweaters, worn by men, were considered underwear. The sweaters were worn over a shirt and tucked into trousers, with a vest and coat worn over the top. Many of these sweaters featured two-color designs because of the extra warmth the second yarn provided, but because the undershirt/sweaters were tucked into trousers, the sweaters featured only one color below the waist to save time and conserve yarn. Luckily for us, Norwegian sweaters became outerwear for everyone, young and old. For some, sweaters—like the Adult Voss Sweater—have become a palette for creative expression, for others a source of pride in Norwegian heritage. You don't have to be Norwegian to love Norwegian knitting, though; you just have to appreciate beauty, warmth, and a little bit of history.

Knitting was a vital skill in Norway. Women used wool that they had processed, beginning with raising sheep, shearing them, carding the wool, and spinning it into yarn. Many Norwegian immigrants living in the American Midwest in the nineteenth century also raised sheep for their warm, soft, durable wool and for meat. Although immigrant women could have purchased ready-knit items or yarn for knitting, they often processed their own wool for yarn. Immigrants believed that hand-spun wool yarn and hand-knit objects were better—warmer and more durable—than what they could buy in the store.

Aside from warmth and durability, knitting was also valued for its beauty. Colorfully embroidered mittens and gloves were worn to church in Norway. In Selbu, near Trondheim, it was a tradition for the bride to give patterned mittens to all the members of her wedding party. Knitting was an expression of creativity and skill. Immigrants brought many of these skills, traditions, and textiles with them when they immigrated to the United States.

When Swedish immigrants came to America, they brought tools and knowledge of practices that provided linens and domestic textiles for families of settlers throughout the Midwest. Swedish textile crafts, including bed coverlets, loom-woven rugs, tablecloths, and runners, are particularly fascinating, and there is a wealth of accessible historical examples in both Sweden and Swedish America. In some areas of Sweden, successive craft traditions have never been broken, spanning centuries of transition from agrarian society to today's twenty-first-century technology.

When 1800s industrialization consumed manpower from traditional households, Swedish textile crafts were generally those that survived. The Handcraft Movement, a reaction to extensive industrial production, redirected attention to home craft production. Textile crafts like loom-woven linen and rugs, spinning, embroidery, and knitting played an important role in the birth of the Handcraft Movement and remain among the strongest

practiced handcraft traditions today in Sweden. Traditional pieces reveal how Swedish traditions were continued in this country and how those traditions influenced textiles more generally in the Midwest.

English, German, or Dutch merchants may have brought knitting to Iceland. Knitting quickly spread throughout the country and soon became the main cottage industry. Everyone was knitting—young and old, men and women—and all were supposed to produce a specified amount of knitted goods over a certain period of time. People were knitting both refined knits on tiny needles for special occasions and more utilitarian garments for their own everyday use. They were also knitting an enormous quantity of goods, probably much rougher and in plain colors, aimed for exportation.

The Icelandic knitting of today conjures up visions of lopi yoke sweaters knit in natural colors, but you won't find any lopi sweaters in the textile museums in Iceland. The reason for that is simple: The "traditional" Icelandic sweater is a

relatively recent invention. In the 1950s, as yoke sweaters became fashionable in the Western world, a yoke sweater with a definite Icelandic flair emerged, and by the 1970s, it was immensely popular. The unspun lopi with which the *lopapeysa*—which literally translates to "sweater in lopi wool"—is knitted is a bit older, dating back to the early 1900s, when "lazy" women began to knit without spinning the wool into yarn first.

And now it has all been gathered in one place: Norwegian mittens, Swedish hats, Icelandic sweaters, and much more. Knit using traditional techniques as you work your way through these contemporary patterns based on historical practice. There is a rich Nordic knitting heritage, and you'll find much of it here in *Nordic Knits*.

NORWEGIAN
HANDKNITS

Norwegian knitting usually conjures up visions of ski sweaters worn by the Scandinavian teams at the Winter Olympics. It was the beauty and relative simplicity of these sweaters that inspired this collection of patterns, much of which came from exhibitions at Norwegian museums that display spinning, nålbinding, Setesdal embroidery, band weaving, bentwood box making, and felt making. Vesterheim is the oldest and most comprehensive museum in the United States dedicated to a single immigrant group, Norwegian Americans; the sheer magnitude of their textiles collection is very impressive: drawers filled with colorful mittens and gloves, racks loaded with incredible embroidered bunads, and rolls of exquisite tapestries.

As knitters, we are the farmers, and the designs in this book are the seeds. And we can nurture these old fiber traditions to ensure they are not forgotten, and help preserve the heritage of the Norwegian people who immigrated to their "western home."

The inspiration for some of the patterns came very naturally by just modifying old designs. Other patterns, such as the Voss Family Sweaters, took extensive study of the artifact and days of graphing various pattern possibilities. The end result is a collection of patterns steeped in Norwegian history that we hope you will enjoy knitting for family and friends.

RUTH'S CAP

This hat was inspired by one made by Mina Elstad Quickstad (1871–1924) for her daughter Ruth. The hat was kept in the family, then was donated to the Vesterheim. This "grown-up" version of this charming cap has small touches of adult sophistication. This cap is perfect for those cold weekend mornings when we in the Midwest get reacquainted with our snowblowers.

SIZE
Adult's average

FINISHED MEASUREMENTS
Circumference: 22½"/57cm

Length: 9½"/24cm

MATERIALS
Dale of Norway *Freestyle* (100% superwash wool, 50g/1.75oz, 87yds/80m per ball): 2 balls Aubergine #5072

Size 7 (4.5mm) double-pointed needles (set of 5) and two 16"/40.5cm circular needles or size needed to obtain gauge

Medium-size crochet hook

Stitch markers, 1 in CC for beg of rnd

Tapestry needle

GAUGE
17 sts and 24 rnds = 4" (10cm) in pat st.

Adjust needle size as necessary to obtain correct gauge.

Pattern Stitch

Ruth's Cap Chart below

Special Technique

Provisional Cast-On: With crochet hook and waste yarn, make a chain several sts longer than desired cast-on. With knitting needle and project yarn, pick up indicated number of sts in the "bumps" on back of chain. When indicated in pattern, "unzip" the crochet chain to free live sts.

Pattern Note

Switch to double-pointed needles when stitches no longer fit comfortably on circular needle.

Instructions

Using provisional method and circular needle, CO 96 sts; pm for beg of rnd and join, taking care not to twist sts.

Knit 10 rnds.

Turning rnd: Purl. Knit 10 rnds.

Unzip provisional cast-on, placing live sts on 2nd circular needle; fold hem at turning rnd so that needles are parallel.

Joining rnd: Using the needle in front, *insert right tip into first st on front needle, then into first st on back needle and knit them tog; rep from * around—96 sts.

Body

Beg with Rnd 2 of chart, work even in pat st for 6", ending with either Rnd 2 or 4; on last rnd, place markers every 6 sts around.

Crown

Dec rnd: Maintaining est pat, *work to 2 sts before marker, k2tog, rep from * around—80 sts.

Next rnd: Work even.

Rep last 2 rnds twice more, working decs at vertical St st ridges—48 sts.

Next rnd: Removing markers, k2tog around—24 sts.

INSPIRED BY
The knit cap that inspired this project was made by Mina Elstad Quickstad for her daughter Ruth (b. Nov. 8, 1891) of Toronto, South Dakota.

Next rnd: Work even.

Next rnd: K2tog around—12 sts.

Break yarn, leaving a 6" tail; thread through rem sts, pull tight, and secure tail to WS.

Finishing

Weave in all ends.

Block to finished measurements.

Make tassel and tail as desired; sew to top of cap.

RUTH'S CAP CHART

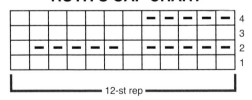

12-st rep

STITCH KEY

	Knit
—	Purl

RUTH'S MITTENS

These mittens are a natural choice for the garter stitch pattern. The garter stitch has a wonderful stretch for a warm, snug, but not tight-fitting mitten. Knit in the spring green *Freestyle* yarn, the mittens bring a promise of new life through the long winter months. Add the ruffle for your favorite snow bunny or ski bum!

SIZE
Adult's average

FINISHED MEASUREMENTS
Circumference (around hand): 8"/20cm

Length: 9"/23cm

MATERIALS 4
Dale of Norway *Freestyle* (100% superwash wool, 50g/1.75oz, 87yds/80m per ball): 2 balls Spring Green #9133

Size 5 (3.75mm) double-pointed needles (set of 5)

Size 7 (4.5mm) double-pointed needles (set of 5) or size needed to obtain gauge

Stitch markers, 1 in CC for beg of rnd

Tapestry needle

GAUGE
17 sts and 24 rnds = 4" (10cm) in pat st with larger needles.

Adjust needle size as necessary to obtain correct gauge.

Special Abbreviations
M1L (Make 1 Left): Insert LH needle from front to back under the running thread between the last st worked and next st on LH needle; knit into the back of resulting loop.

M1R (Make 1 Right): Insert LH needle from back to front under the running thread between the last st worked and next st on LH needle; knit into the front of resulting loop.

N1, N2, N3, N4: Needles 1, 2, 3, 4

Instructions
Right Mitten

Ruffled Cuff
With smaller needles, CO 68 sts and distribute on 4 dpns; pm for beg of rnd and join, taking care not to twist sts.

Knit 2 rnds.

Dec rnd: K2tog around—34 sts.

Work 14 rnds in K1, p1 Rib.

Thumb Gusset
Change to larger needles.

Work Rnd 1 of chart and inc 2 sts evenly around— 36 sts.

Work 4 rnds even following chart, and on last rnd, pm after first st for thumb gusset.

Inc rnd: M1R, knit to marker, M1L, slip marker, work in est pat around—38 sts.

Next rnd: Work even, working St st between beg of rnd and thumb gusset markers and maintaining pat on all other sts.

Rep [last 2 rnds] 7 times, then rep Inc rnd once more—54 sts, with 19 sts in thumb gusset section.

Next rnd: Slip 19 thumb gusset sts to waste yarn, CO 1 above opening, work in est pat around—36 sts.

Main Mitten

Rearrange sts so that there are 9 sts on each of the 4 dpns.

Work even in est pat for 3" (or 2" short of desired finished length), ending with Rnd 3 or 4.

Top Decrease

Dec rnd: N1: K1, ssk, work in pat to end; N2: work in pat to last 3 sts, k2tog, k1; N3 and N4: work as for N1 and N2—32 sts.

Next rnd: Work even in est pat.

Rep [last 2 rnds] 4 more times—16 sts.

Break yarn, leaving a 6" tail; thread tail through rem sts, pull tight, and secure tail to WS.

Thumb

Slip the 19 sts from waste yarn to 3 larger dpns.

Rnd 1: Beg at 1-st CO, pick up and knit 1 st, knit to end, then pick up and knit 1 st—21 sts.

Rnd 2: K2tog, knit to last 2 sts, k2tog—19 sts.

Work even for 8 rnds or until thumb section reaches beg of your thumbnail.

Dec rnd: K1, *k2tog, k1; rep from * around—13 sts.

Next rnd 2: Knit.

Rep last 2 rnds once more—9 sts.

Next rnd: [K2tog, k1] 3 times—3 sts.

Break yarn, leaving a 6" tail; thread tail through rem sts, pull tight, and secure tail to WS.

Left Mitten

Work as for Right Mitten to Inc rnd for thumb gusset, but on last rnd, place markers following 18th and 19th sts for thumb gusset.

Inc rnd: Work in est pat to first marker, slip marker, M1R, knit to 2nd marker, M1L, slip marker, work in est pat to end of rnd—38 sts.

Next rnd: Work even, working St st between thumb gusset markers and maintaining pat on all other sts.

Rep [last 2 rnds] 7 times, then rep Inc rnd once more—54 sts, with 19 sts in thumb gusset section.

Next rnd: Work in est pat to marker, slip 19 thumb gusset sts to waste yarn, CO 1 above opening, work in est pat around—36 sts.

Cont as for Right Mitten.

Finishing

Weave in all ends. Block as necessary.

RUTH'S MITTEN CHART

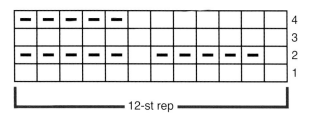

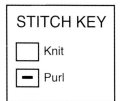

STITCH KEY

☐ Knit

▬ Purl

12-st rep

NISSE HATS

A *nisse* is a Norwegian folklore elf with childlike appeal and is recognized by his red stocking cap. When Hitler's troops occupied Norway during World War II, some Norwegians wore a nisse-style red stocking cap as a sign of defiance. A tapestry weaving by Pauline Fjelde from the original Luther College Collection provided inspiration for the nisse Hats. The hat can be made for a child, for the child's favorite stuffed animal, or for an egg.

SIZES
Child (Teddy bear, egg)

Instructions are written for largest size with smaller sizes in parentheses. When only 1 number is given, it applies to all sizes.

FINISHED MEASUREMENT
Circumference: 17 (8, 6)"/43 (20, 15)cm

MATERIALS ⚙1
Dale of Norway *Baby Ull* (100% superwash merino wool, 180yds/50g per skein): 2 (1, 1) skein(s) Red #4018

Size 2 (2.75mm) 16"/40.5cm circular and/or double-pointed needles (set of 5) or size needed to obtain gauge

Stitch markers, 1 in CC for beg of rnd

Tapestry needle

GAUGE
32 sts and 44 rnds = 4" (10cm) in St st.

Adjust needle size as necessary to obtain correct gauge.

INSPIRED BY
The Elves tapestry, Luther College Collection. Pauline Fjelde wove *The Elves* tapestry in 1892 in Minneapolis, Minnesota. Pauline (1861–1923) was born in Ålesund, Norway, and immigrated to Minneapolis in 1887. Pauline was also well known for her embroidery; she and her sister, Thomane, embroidered the first Minnesota state flag.

Pattern Note
For Child's hat, begin with circular needle, then change to double-pointed needles when stitches no longer fit comfortably on the circular needle; for smaller-size hats, use double-pointed needles throughout.

Instructions

CO 136 (64, 48) sts; pm for beg of rnd and join, being careful not to twist sts.

Work even in St st (knit all rnds) until piece measures 6 (2, 1)".

Next rnd: *K17 (8, 6), pm; rep from * around.

Dec rnd: *Knit to 2 sts before marker, k2tog; rep from * around—128 (56, 40) sts rem.

Knit 4 rnds even.

Rep [last 5 rnds] 14 (5, 3) times—16 sts.

Next rnd: K2tog around—8 sts.

Knit 2 rnds.

Break yarn, leaving a 6" tail; using tapestry needle, thread tail through rem sts, pull tight, and secure.

Finishing

Weave in all ends. Block to finished measurements.

"LEATHER" WAIST POUCH

The waist pouch was commonly used by men and is considered a remnant of the Middle Ages, when garments did not have pockets. This knit version of a leather waist pouch can be made as a small bag with a shoulder strap or with belt loops to be worn at the waist.

FINISHED MEASUREMENTS
6"/15cm x 7"/18cm (excluding strap)

MATERIALS 4
Cascade Yarns *220* (100% wool, 100g/3.5oz, 220yds/201m per skein): 1 skein Rust Heather #2435

Size 10½ (6.5mm) double-pointed needles (set of 5) and 16"/40.5cm circular needles or size needed to obtain gauge

Tapestry needle

Stitch markers (1 in CC for beg of rnd)

¾"/1.9cm pewter button or felted-ball button

Paternayan yarn from JCA for embroidery, 100% Persian Wool, 8-yd skein 8–10 various colors

PRE-FULLED GAUGE
15 sts and 20 rnds = 4" (10cm) in St st with single strand of yarn.

Gauge is not critical for this project; make sure that your sts are loose and airy.

Pattern Notes
The pouch is worked in the round from top to bottom; change to double-pointed needles when stitches no longer fit comfortably on circular needle.

The pouch flap is worked back and forth.

Embroidery is done after fulling to finished size.

Instructions
Pouch
With single strand, CO 48 sts onto circular needle, pm for beg of rnd and join, taking care not to twist sts.

Rnd 1: K24, pm, k24.

Rnds 2–5: Knit.

Rnd 6: *Slip marker, k1, M1, knit to 1 st before marker, M1, k1, rep from * around—52 sts.

Rnds 7–8: Knit.

Rnds 9–23: Rep [Rnds 6–8] 5 times—72 sts.

Rnds 24–31: Knit.

Rnd 32: *Slip marker, k1, ssk, knit to 3 sts before marker, k2tog, k1, rep from * around—68 sts.

Rnd 33: Knit.

Rep [Rnds 32 and 33] 15 times—8 sts.

Break yarn; using tapestry needle, thread tail through rem sts, pull tight, and secure end.

Flap
With RS facing, pick up and knit 24 sts along back of cast-on edge.

Row 1 (WS): K2, purl to last 2 sts, k2.

Row 2: Knit.

Rows 3 and 5: K2, purl to last 2 sts, k2.

Row 4: K2, M1, knit to last 2 sts, M1, k2—26 sts.

Row 6: Knit.

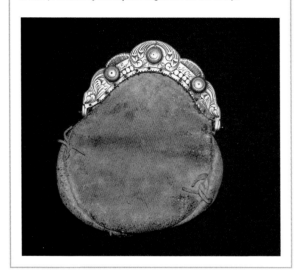

Row 7: K2, M1, purl to last 2 sts, M1, k2—28 sts.

Row 8: Knit.

Rows 9–14: Rep Rows 3–8—32 sts.

Row 15: K2, purl to last 2 sts, k2.

Row 16: K2, ssk, knit to last 4 sts, k2tog, k2—30 sts.

Rep [Rows 15 and 16] 8 times—14 sts.

Rep Row 15 once more.

Buttonhole Row: K2, ssk, k1, k2tog, [yo] twice, ssk, k1, k2tog, k2—12 sts.

Knitting in front and back of double yo on next row, rep [Rows 16 and 15] 3 times—6 sts.

BO and secure end of yarn.

Option 1: I-Cord Purse Strap
With dpns, CO 5 sts.

Row 1: K5; do not turn; slide sts to opposite end of needle.

Rep Row 1 until I-cord measures 78".

BO and secure end of yarn.

Sew ends to sides of purse.

Option 2: I-Cord Belt Bag Straps (make 2)

With dpns, CO 5 sts.

Row 1: K5; do not turn; slide sts to opposite end of needle.

Rep Row 1 until I-cord measures 4".

BO and secure end of yarn.

Sew one end to top edge of back and other end to middle of back.

Weave in all ends.

Finishing

Full purse until it reaches finished measurements or desired size.

Embroidery

When purse is completely dry, embroider as follows: Work solid sections in satin stitch, following the template. Use stem stitch or backstitch to outline solid sections once they have been competed.

Sew button on bag opposite buttonhole.

EMBROIDERY TEMPLATE

ROSEMALED SHAG BAG

This sturdy bag is knit with a double strand of yarn prior to fulling. Needle felting is used to apply the design since the thickness of the finished bag is much too stiff for hand embroidery.

The idea of adding shag around the top rim of the bag came from a pair of gloves that were from the collection of weaver and world traveler Ruth Ketterer Harris and her husband, Wilfred. Based on the embroidery motifs and colors, the gloves were most likely made in the early twentieth century in Numedal, Buskerud County, Norway.

The familiar *rosemaled* motif was inspired by the embroidery on a pair of mittens that featured four similar motifs. Betsey Toifson Hansen (1867–1958) brought the mittens from Hallingdal, Norway, to Linn Grove, Iowa, in about 1875.

FINISHED MEASUREMENTS (AFTER FULLING)
Circumference: 28"/71cm

Length: 13"/33cm

MATERIALS 4
Cascade Yarns *220* (100% wool, 100g/3.5oz, 220yds/201m per skein): 5 skeins Teal #8892 (MC)

4 colors of contrasting yarns for needle-felted motif; approx 3 yards/2.7m of each

Size 10½ (6.5mm) 16" /40.5cm circular needles

Size 15 (10mm) double-pointed and 24"/60.9cm circular needles

Tapestry needle

Stitch markers, 1 in CC for beg of rnd

Needle-felting needle

PRE-FULLED GAUGE
13 sts and 18 rnds = 4" (10cm) in St st with larger needles and 2 strands of yarn held tog.

Gauge is not critical for this project; make sure your sts are loose and airy.

Special Techniques

5-St I-Cord: *K5, do not turn, slip sts back to LH needle; rep from * until cord is desired length. BO.

Fulling: See page 185.

Pattern Notes

Use double strand of MC throughout construction of the bag.

Bag is worked in the round; change to double-pointed needles when stitches no longer fit comfortably on circular needle.

The template for the *rosemaled* motif is shown in the colors used on the sample. Use whatever colors you desire with whatever yarn you have handy—yarn weight is not an issue.

Needle felting and shag decoration is done after the bag has been fulled to the desired size.

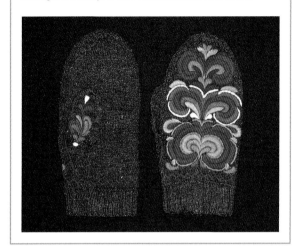

INSPIRED BY

Mittens brought by Betsey Toifson Hansen (1867–1958) from Hallingdal, Norway, to Linn Grove, Iowa, in about 1875.

Instructions

With smaller needles and a double strand of yarn, CO 72 sts; pm for beg of rnd and join, taking care not to twist sts.

Knit 14 rnds.

Next rnd (dec): *K1, k2tog; rep from * around—48 sts.

Next rnd (inc): Change to larger needles; knit in the front and back of each st around—96 sts.

Knit every rnd until piece measures 16" from beg.

Setup rnd: *K8, pm; rep from * around.

Dec rnd: *Knit to 2 sts before marker, k2tog; rep from * around— 84 sts.

Knit 6 rnds, then rep Dec rnd—72 sts.

Knit 5 rnds, then rep Dec rnd—60 sts.

Knit 4 rnds, then rep Dec rnd—48 sts.

Knit 3 rnds, then rep Dec rnd—36 sts.

Knit 2 rnds, then rep Dec rnd—24 sts.

Knit 1 rnd.

Last rnd: K2tog around—12 sts.

Break yarn, leaving a 12" tail; using tapestry needle, thread tail through rem sts and pull tight.

Weave in all ends.

Straps

(make 2)

With a double strand of yarn and larger dpn, CO 5 sts and work I-cord for 48".

Sew to top of bag in "U" shape before fulling.

Finishing

Full the bag in washing machine until it reaches finished measurements or desired size.

Apply shag to rim of bag (see page 24 for instructions).

Following template, needle-felt *rosemaled* motif on bag (see illustration and sidebar on page 23).

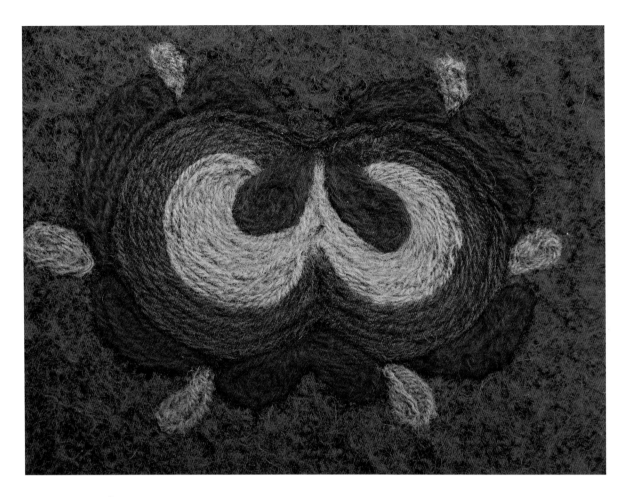

Needle Felting

Stuff the bag with something soft, such as an old sweater; this will prevent you from poking yourself with the needle-felting needle.

Apply four colors of yarn (using the same colors you chose for the shag) to the surface of the felted fabric in the pattern shown in the Rosemaled Template. "Swirling" the yarns into the shapes looks good.

Using the barbed needle-felting needle, repeatedly poke the yarn and fabric until the fibers of the applied yarn have bonded with the fabric of the bag. It may take numerous poking repetitions to get the fiber to bond tightly to the bag.

TEMPLATE FOR NEEDLE-FELTED ROSEMALED ON SHAG BAG

Shag Directions

The shag is applied to the rim of the bag after the fulling process is completed. Four colors (A, B, C, D) are used to create a pattern; the colors used are "knitter's choice."

Lay a pencil or a size 10 dpn along the rim as shown in Step 1 photo. Using a sharp tapestry needle and a double strand of yarn, stitch through the bag and around the needle to make a loop.

Repeat this about 16 times or until the width of the rim is covered (Step 2 photo).

Create loop pattern as follows:

Columns 1 and 2: 16A

Column 3: 16B

Column 4: 6C, 4D, 6C

Repeat Columns 1–4 around the rim of the bag.

Using sharp-tipped scissors, slide blade into center of loops and clip them as shown in Step 3 photo.

Step 1

Step 2

Step 3

NORDIC KNITS

CROSS-COUNTRY SKI HAT

One of our favorite items in this Norwegian handknits collection is a pair of blue-and-white Nordic ski socks. The socks are well worn, or well loved, depending upon your point of view. The frayed areas and holes do not take away from the fact that they are beautifully crafted.

The patterning on the calf gusset was the first thing to grab our designer's eye. Its diminishing diamond pattern was perfect for the crown of a hat. The alternating snowflake patterns on the sock included one very common eight-point star and another not-so-common four-diamond motif that is used in the main band of the hat.

SIZE
Adult's average

FINISHED MEASUREMENTS
Inside circumference: 20"/51cm

Length (brim to crown): 9½"/24cm

MATERIALS 2
Dale of Norway *Heilo* (100% wool, 50g/1.75oz, 109yds/100m per skein): Green/Gold colorway: 2 skeins Olive #8972 (MC) and 1 skein Goldenrod #2427 (CC)

Size 4 (3.5mm) 16"/40.5cm circular needle

Size 5 (3.75mm) double-pointed needles (set of 5) and 16"/40.5cm circular needles or size needed to obtain gauge

Size F/5 (3.75mm) crochet hook

Stitch marker

Tapestry needle

GAUGE
24 sts and 26 rnds = 4" (10cm) in stranded 2-color St st with larger needles.

Adjust needle size as necessary to obtain correct gauge.

Special Techniques

Provisional Cast-On: With crochet hook and waste yarn, make a chain several sts longer than desired cast-on. With knitting needle and project yarn, pick up indicated number of sts in the "bumps" on back of chain. When indicated in pattern, "unzip" the crochet chain to free live sts.

Pattern Notes

The hat is worked in the round; change to double-pointed needles when stitches no longer fit comfortably on circular needle.

The facing is worked on a smaller needle to get a tighter fit; after brim pattern is complete, the facing is folded inside hat and fused to brim using a 3-needle join technique.

INSPIRED BY
Sock, no history available.
Luther College Collection

Instructions

Facing

With smaller needle and MC, using provisional method, CO 130 sts; pm for beg of rnd and join, taking care not to twist sts.

Knit 26 rnds.

Next 2 rnds (turning ridge): Purl.

Brim

Change to larger needle.

Knit 1 rnd.

Work 21 rnds following Chart A.

Next rnd (3-needle join): Place CO sts on smaller needle and fold facing inside brim so that WS are together. (The larger needle with brim sts should be on the outside and the smaller needle with facing sts should be lined up on the inside of the hat). Holding needles parallel and using MC, *knit tog 1 st from the front needle and 1 from the back needle; rep from * around until all sts are joined.

Next 3 rnds: With MC, purl and inc 2 sts evenly spaced on the last rnd—132 sts.

Crown

With MC, knit 1 rnd.

Work 18 rnds following Chart B.

Rnd 19 (dec): Maintaining the charted pat throughout decreasing, *k1, ssk, k7, k2tog; rep from * around—110 sts.

Rnds 20–26: Work even.

Rnd 27 (dec): *K1, ssk, k5, k2tog; rep from * around—88 sts.

Rnds 28–33: Work even.

Rnd 34 (dec): *K1, ssk, k3, k2tog; rep from * around—66 sts.

Rnds 35–38: Work even.

Rnd 39 (dec): *K1, ssk, k1, k2tog; rep from * around—44 sts.

Rnd 40: Work even. Break CC.

Rnd 41 (dec): *K1, S2KP2; rep from * around—22 sts.

Rnd 42: Knit.

Break yarn, leaving a 6" tail.

With tapestry needle, thread tail through rem sts, pull tight, and leave tail for securing braided tassel.

Braided Tassel

Cut 12 [16] pieces of MC and 8 [16] pieces of CC.

Create two bundles of yarn with 6 MC and 4 CC in each bundle. Tie one end of the bundle and make fishtail braid until 2" of yarn rem. Tie overhand knot. Rep for 2nd braid. Fold both braids in half using tail at top of hat, secure to hat.

Finishing

Weave in all ends. Block to finished measurements.

CROSS-COUNTRY SKI HAT CHARTS

CHART A: BRIM

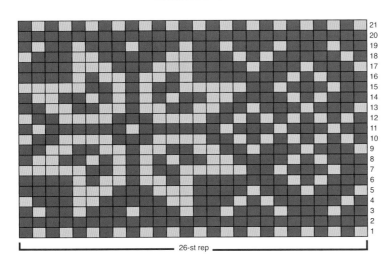

26-st rep

STITCH AND COLOR KEY

- Knit MC
- Knit CC
- K2tog MC
- Ssk MC
- S2KP2 MC

CHART B: CROWN

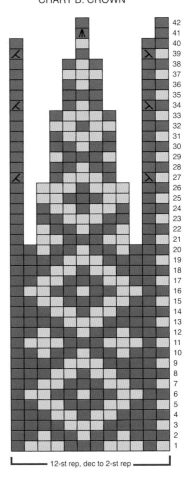

12-st rep, dec to 2-st rep

ROSE OR BRIDAL WIMPLE

The wimple has its origins in the Near East and was worn as a fashion accessory by women in medieval Europe following the Crusades. It survives to this day as part of the habits worn by nuns from certain orders. Modern women living in chilly northern climates also wear wimples to keep warm in the winter.

The two charted design choices are from some of the many Selbu mittens at Vesterheim.

FINISHED MEASUREMENTS
Circumference (main section): Approx. 26"/66cm

Length: Approx. 21"/53cm

MATERIALS 🧶1🧶
Rose version: Raumagarn Røros Lamullgarn (100% wool, 50g/1.75oz, 273yds/250m per skein): 4 skeins Light Gray #12 (2 strands held together = MC); 1 skein each Light Blue #67 and Medium Blue #68 (blues held tog = CC)

🧶2🧶 **Bridal version:** Misti International *Misti Alpaca Sport* (100% alpaca; 50g/1.75oz, 146yds/134m per skein): 3 skeins Natural Dark Brown #NT408 (MC) and 1 skein Golden Spice #MR6213

Size 6 (4mm) 24"/60cm circular needle or 1 size smaller than size needed to obtain gauge

Size 7 (4.5mm) 24"/60cm circular needle or size needed to obtain gauge

Stitch markers, 1 in CC for beg of rnd

Tapestry needle

GAUGE
20 sts and 22 rnds = 4" (10cm) in stranded 2-color St st with larger needle; for Rose version, 2 strands of yarn are held tog throughout.

Adjust needle size as necessary to obtain correct gauge.

INSPIRED BY
These gloves (ca. 1900) belonged to Lully Hansen Lund, who immigrated from Drammen, Norway, to Fargo, North Dakota, in 1919.

Pattern Stitch

Lace (multiple of 8 sts)

Rnd 1: [K1, yo, k1, k2tog, p1, ssk, k1, yo] 26 times.

Rnd 2: [K4, p1, k3] 26 times.

Rep Rnds 1 and 2 for pat.

Pattern Notes

The Rose version is worked with two strands of yarn held together; the two blue yarns held together create the contrasting color (CC).

If desired, place markers between each lace repeat.

Take care with tension when working stranded stockinette stitch; if necessary, change to smaller needle size when working plain stockinette stitch to match gauge of pattern section.

Instructions

Lace Border

With larger needle and MC, CO 208 sts; pm for beg of rnd and join, taking care not to twist sts.

Purl 1 rnd.

Work 24 rnds in lace pat.

Main Section

Knit 1 rnd, placing markers every 13 sts.

Dec rnd: *Knit to 2 sts before marker, k2tog; rep from * around—192 sts.

Next rnd: Knit.

Rep [last 2 rnds] 3 times more—144 sts.

Rose version only

Next rnd: *Knit to marker, [knit to 2 sts before next marker, k2tog] 7 times; rep from * once more—130 sts.

Bridal version only

Next rnd: Rep Dec rnd—128 sts.

Knit 1 rnd, rearranging markers as follows: *Rose pat:* every 13 sts; *Bridal pat:* every 16 sts.

Work chart for either Roses or Bridal pat as desired, removing markers on last rnd.

With MC, work even in St st until piece measures 15" from end of lace pat or to desired length.

With smaller needle, work k1, p1 Rib for 1".

Bind off very loosely in rib.

Finishing

Weave in all ends.

Block to finished measurements, opening up lace section as desired.

BRIDAL CHART
FOR WIMPLE AND WRISTER

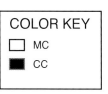

COLOR KEY

☐ MC

■ CC

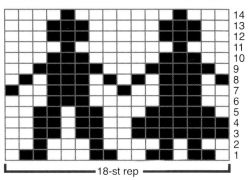

14
13
12
11
10
9
8
7
6
5
4
3
2
1

⊢—— 18-st rep ——⊣

ROSE CHART
FOR WIMPLE AND WRISTER

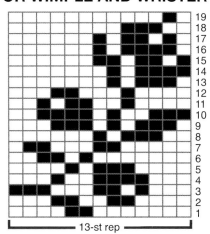

19
18
17
16
15
14
13
12
11
10
9
8
7
6
5
4
3
2
1

⊢—— 13-st rep ——⊣

LACE CHART

STITCH KEY

☐ Knit

— Purl

O Yo

／ K2tog

＼ Ssk

⊢— 8-st rep —⊣

DANCING HAT

This traditional hat was made for a man named Oddgeir, who was a member of a traditional Norwegian dancing troupe. It was knit by his mother from what she had on hand because the cream color appears to be knit in a cotton thread, providing an interesting contrast to the wool used for the rest of the hat. The new hat differs from the original in the hem treatment—the original was topstitched in a Bargello style of stitching, while the new version has a knitted-in color hem in the flavor of the original. We think Oddgeir's mother would have approved. While knitting this hat, try daydreaming about traditional Nordic dancing, and you might find your feet tapping in time to your needles!

SIZE
Adult's average

FINISHED MEASUREMENTS
Circumference at head: Approx. 22"/56cm

Length (not including pom-pom): Approx. 14"/36cm

MATERIALS 【2】
Reynolds *Whiskey* (100% Shetland wool, 50g/1.75oz, 195yds/178m per ball): 1 ball each Navy #3608 (MC), Gold #101 (A), Acid Green #103 (B), Red #011 (C), Mushroom #031 (D), and Dark Green #059 (E)

Size 1 (2.25mm) double-pointed needles (set of 5) and two 16"/40.5cm circular needles or size needed to obtain gauge

Small crochet hook

Stitch markers, 1 in CC for beg of rnd

Tapestry needle

Pom-pom maker (optional)

GAUGE
35 sts and 37 rnds = 4" (10cm) in stranded St st.

Adjust needle size as necessary to obtain correct gauge.

Special Technique

Provisional Cast-On: With crochet hook and waste yarn, make a chain several sts longer than desired cast-on. With knitting needle and project yarn, pick up indicated number of sts in the "bumps" on back of chain. When indicated in pattern, "unzip" the crochet chain to free live sts.

Pattern Notes

Change to double-pointed needles when stitches no longer fit comfortably on circular needle.

Take care with tension when working stranded stockinette stitch; if necessary, change to smaller needle size when working plain stockinette stitch to match gauge of color pattern sections.

Instructions

Border and Hem

With circular needle and MC, using provisional method, CO 192 sts; pm for beg of rnd and join, taking care not to twist sts.

Knit 8 rnds.

Turning rnd: Purl.

Work 8 rnds following Bargello chart.

Remove provisional cast-on and place live sts on 2nd circular needle; fold work along turning rnd so that needles are parallel.

Joining rnd: Using the needle in front and MC, *insert right tip into first st on front needle, then into first st on back needle and knit them tog; rep from * around—192 sts.

Body of Hat

Knit 1 rnd and inc 6 st evenly around—198 sts.

Work even in St st for 2¼".

Work 37 rnds following Grand Star Chart.

Next rnd (dec): With MC, *k31, k2tog; rep from * around—192 sts.

Knit 1 rnd, placing markers every 24 sts.

Dec rnd: *Knit to 2 sts before marker, k2tog; rep from * around— 184 sts.

Cont in St st and rep Dec rnd [every other rnd] 5 times—144 sts.

Knit 1 rnd, removing markers.

Work 27 rnds following North Star Chart.

With MC, knit 1 rnd, placing markers every 24 sts.

Cont in St st and work Dec rnd on next, then [every other rnd] 7 times—96 sts.

Knit 1 rnd, removing markers.

Next rnd: [K14, k2tog] twice, k30, [k2tog, k14] twice, k2—92 sts.

Knit 1 rnd.

Work 9 rnds following Little Dipper Chart.

Change to MC and knit 1 rnd.

Next rnd: Knit and dec 2 sts evenly around, placing markers every 15 sts—90 sts.

Work Dec rnd on next, then [every other rnd] 10 times—24 sts.

Knit 1 rnd, removing markers.

Break yarn, leaving a 10" tail; thread tail through rem sts, pull tight, then secure to WS.

Finishing

Weave in all ends. Block to finished measurements.

Pom-Pom

Use pom-pom maker or follow instructions as follows:

Cut 2 cardboard circles the size of desired pom-pom. Cut a hole in the center of each circle, approx ½" in diameter. Thread a tapestry needle with one very long strand each of all colors. Holding both circles together, insert needle through center hole, over the outside edge, through center again, going around and around until entire circle is covered and center hole is filled (thread more length of yarn as needed). With sharp scissors, cut yarn between the 2 circles all around the circumference. Using 2 [12"] strands of yarn (tying ends), wrap yarn between circles, going 2 or 3 times around; pull tight and tie into a firm knot. Remove cardboard and fluff out pom-pom. Trim ends as necessary to make pom-pom circular. Attach pom-pom to hat using tying ends.

INSPIRED BY
The original hat was worn by Oddgeir Fletre, immigrant from Hardanger, Norway, when dancing with Leikarringen Heimhug in Chicago in the 1950s.

DANCING HAT CHARTS

LITTLE DIPPER

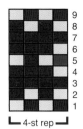

9
8
7
6
5
4
3
2
1

└─ 4-st rep ─┘

BARGELLO BAND

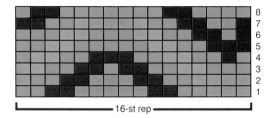

8
7
6
5
4
3
2
1

├──────── 16-st rep ────────┤

NORTH STAR

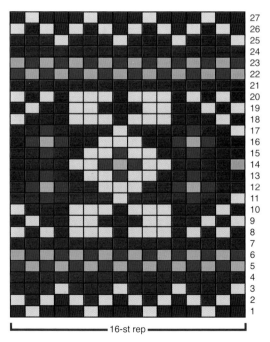

27
26
25
24
23
22
21
20
19
18
17
16
15
14
13
12
11
10
9
8
7
6
5
4
3
2
1

├──────── 16-st rep ────────┤

GRAND STAR

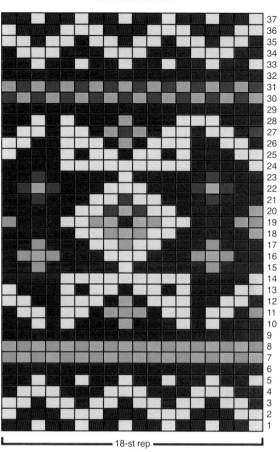

37
36
35
34
33
32
31
30
29
28
27
26
25
24
23
22
21
20
19
18
17
16
15
14
13
12
11
10
9
8
7
6
5
4
3
2
1

├──────── 18-st rep ────────┤

COLOR KEY

- Navy (MC)
- Gold (A)
- Acid Green (B)
- Red (C)
- Mushroom (D)
- Dark Green (E)

FLOWER HAT WITH EARFLAPS

The flower motif on this hat was inspired by a pair of mittens that featured an unusual mix of a flower pattern and a snowflake pattern. It is interesting to note that what most of us refer to as a traditional Norwegian snowflake design was intended to represent a flower. The original mittens were knit by an immigrant's mother in 1911. The name of the immigrant and the mother are unknown since the mitten came to Vesterheim by way of an antique dealer. The mittens are from the Sunnfjord region of Norway, which is north of Bergen.

SIZE
Adult's average

FINISHED MEASUREMENTS
Circumference: 20"/50cm

Length (including earflaps):
    12"/30cm

MATERIALS
Dale of Norway *Falk* (100%
    superwash wool, 50g/1.75oz,
    116yds/106m per ball): 1 ball each
    Cocoa (MC) and Turquoise (CC)

Size 4 (3.5mm) double-pointed
    needles (set of 5) and
    16"/40.5cm circular needles or
    size needed to obtain gauge

Size E/4 (3.5mm) or F/5 (3.75mm)
    crochet hook

Stitch markers, 1 in CC for beg
    of rnd

Tapestry needle

GAUGE
24 sts and 30 rnds = 4" (10cm) in
    stranded 2-color St st.

*Adjust needle size as necessary to
    obtain correct gauge.*

Pattern Notes

Crochet picot cast-on is used to make the picot edging at the cuff; crochet picot bind-off is used to make the edging around the earflaps (see Crochet Picot Cast-On on page 183).

The color pattern is worked using the "stranded" method, i.e., by carrying both colors at once. Avoid long floats on the inside of the hat in those areas where more than five consecutive stitches are worked in one color by catching the color not in use with the working color.

Decreases are worked within the two-color pattern and are indicated on the charts.

Change to dpns when stitches no longer fit comfortably on the circular needle.

Earflaps are worked separately and sewn on.

Instructions

Edging

With circular needle and CC, CO 120 sts using the crochet picot method as follows: crochet CO 2 sts, *chain 3 sts to make picot loop, join loop, crochet CO 3 sts over needle; rep from * (119 sts), end with [chain 3, join loop, place loop from crochet hook onto needle] for the last st, pm for beg of rnd and join, taking care not to twist sts.

Rnd 1: (CC) Purl.

Rnd 2: Join MC and knit.

Rnd 3: (MC) Purl.

Rnds 4 and 6: (CC) Knit.

Rnds 5 and 7: (CC) Purl.

Rnd 8: (MC) Knit and place markers every 20 sts.

Body

Work 20 rnds of Chart A and on last rnd, work color pat and dec as follows: *k5, ssk, k5, k2tog, k6; rep from * around—108 sts.

Work 13 rnds of Chart B and on last rnd, work color pat and dec as follows: *k3, ssk, k7, k2tog, k4; rep from * around—96 sts.

Work 12 rnds of Chart C and on Rnd 9, work color pat and dec as follows: *k2, ssk, k7, k2tog, k3; rep from * around; break off CC after chart is complete—84 sts.

Crown

Dec rnd: With MC, *ssk, knit to 3 sts from marker, ktog, k1; rep from * around—72 sts.

Continue in St st and rep Dec rnd [every other rnd] 4 times, ending with Dec rnd—24 sts.

Break yarn, leaving 6" tail.

With tapestry needle, thread yarn through rem sts, and pull tight; secure tail on WS.

Earflap (make 2)

With dpns and MC, CO 17 sts.

Work 18 rows of Earflap Chart, working decs on Rows 14 and 16 as follows: working in color pat, k1, ssk, work to last 3 sts, k2tog, k1.

Slip rem 13 sts to holder.

Earflap Edging

With RS facing and using CC, pick up and knit 12 sts along one edge of earflap, k13 sts from holder, pick up and knit another 12 sts along other edge.

Knit 1 row with CC, then knit 2 rows MC, and 2 rows CC.

With CC, work crochet picot BO as follows: With crochet hook in right hand and needle in left hand, use crochet hook to BO 1 st, *chain 3, join loop by working sc into last st on needle; BO 3; rep from * around.

Break yarn, leaving a 15" tail.

Pull yarn through rem st.

With tapestry needle and tail, sew earflap to hat.

Finishing

Weave in loose ends. Block to finished measurements.

FLOWER HAT CHARTS

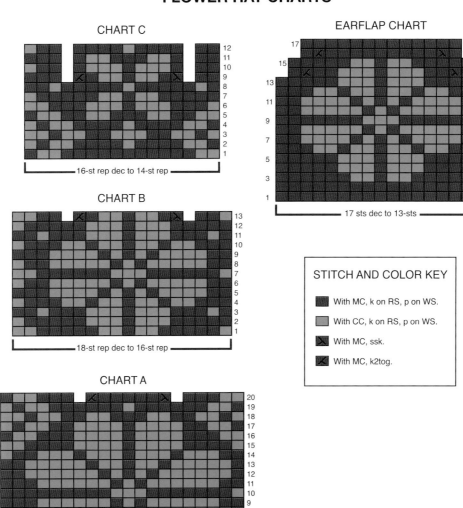

CHART C

16-st rep dec to 14-st rep

CHART B

18-st rep dec to 16-st rep

CHART A

20-st rep dec to 18-st rep

EARFLAP CHART

17 sts dec to 13-sts

STITCH AND COLOR KEY

■ With MC, k on RS, p on WS.

■ With CC, k on RS, p on WS.

✕ With MC, ssk.

✕ With MC, k2tog.

FLOWER MITTENS

Knit a pair of mittens featuring the same flower and snowflake motif as the earflap hat.
The original mittens were made of hand-spun wool.

SIZE
Women's average

FINISHED MEASUREMENTS
Circumference: 8½"/22cm

Length: 11"/28cm

MATERIALS
Dale of Norway *Falk* (100% superwash wool,
 50g/1.75oz, 116yds/106m per ball): 1 ball each Cocoa
 #3072 (MC) and Turquoise #6027 (CC)

Size 4 (3.5mm) double-pointed needles (set of 5) or
 size needed to obtain gauge

Stitch markers, 1 in CC for beg of rnd

Tapestry needle

GAUGE
24 sts and 30 rnds = 4" (10cm) in stranded 2-color St st.

*Adjust needle size as necessary to obtain correct
 gauge.*

Special Abbreviation
S2KP2: Slip 2 sts tog knitwise, k1, pass the
slipped sts over; this is a centered double decrease.

Pattern Notes
After working the cuff, follow the appropriate
color charts throughout and shape as indicated.

The color pattern is worked using the "stranded"
method, i.e., by carrying both colors at once.
Avoid long floats on the inside of the mitten
in those areas where more than 5 consecutive
stitches are worked in one color by catching the
color not in use with the working color.

The main chart shows the left-hand mitten; to
make a right-hand mitten, work Rnds 1–11 of the
Right Palm Chart (below the main chart), then
continue with the main chart.

Instructions
Left Mitten

Cuff
With MC, CO 44 sts and distribute evenly on 4 dpns; pm for beg of rnd and join, taking care not to twist sts.

Work 12 rnds of k1, p1 Rib.

Join CC and continuing in est rib, work stripes as follows: 1 rnd CC, 1 rnd MC, 1 rnd CC, 2 rnds MC, 2 rnds CC, 2 rnds MC, 1 rnd CC, 1 rnd MC, 1 rnd CC [break CC], 6 rnds MC.

Thumb Gusset
Setup rnd: With MC, k40, pm, k3, pm, k1.

Rnd 1: Join CC and beg Mitten Chart.

Rnds 2, 4, 6, 8 (inc): Knit to marker, slip marker, M1, knit to marker, M1, slip marker, k1—2 sts inc'd each rnd, with 11 sts between markers on Rnd 8.

Rnd 3 and all odd rnds: Work even.

Rnd 10: Knit to marker, remove markers, and slip 11 sts between markers to waste yarn or holder, CO 11 sts in *pat* to create thumb opening, knit to end of rnd—52 sts.

Main Mitten
Work even for 28 rnds and on last rnd, place marker after 26th st.

Top Decrease
Dec rnd: *K1, ssk, work to 2 sts before marker, k2tog, rep from * once—48 sts.

Rep Dec rnd [every rnd] 10 more times—8 sts.

Next rnd: [K1, S2KP2] twice—4 sts.

Break yarn, leaving 6" tails.

With tapestry needle, thread yarn through rem sts, and pull tight; secure tails on WS.

Thumb
Slip 11 thumb gusset sts back to needle; with MC, pick up 13 sts around the thumb opening, pm for beg of rnd—24 sts.

Join CC and work Thumb Chart for 17 rnds, placing marker after 12th st on last rnd.

Dec rnd: *K1, ssk, knit to 2 sts before marker, k2tog, rep from * around—20 sts.

Rep Dec rnd [every rnd] 3 more times—8 sts.

Next rnd: [K1, S2KP2] twice—4 sts.

Break yarn, leaving 6" tails.

With tapestry needle, thread yarn through rem sts, and pull tight; secure tails on WS.

Right Mitten
Work cuff as for Left Mitten.

Thumb Gusset
Setup rnd: With MC, k28, pm, k3, pm, k13.

Work as for Right Mitten but follow Left Palm Chart for thumb gusset.

When finished with thumb gusset, complete as for Right Mitten.

Finishing
Weave in ends and block as necessary.

FLOWER MITTEN CHARTS

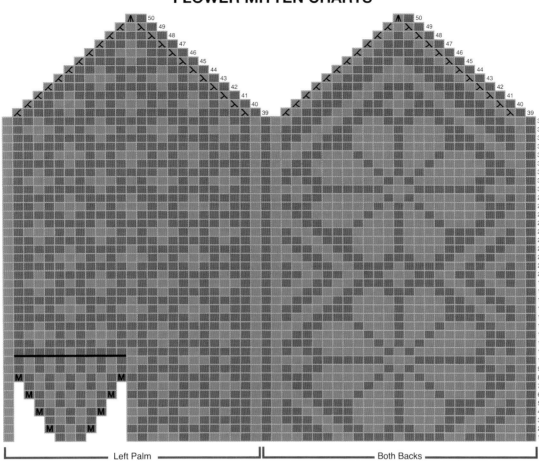

Left Palm — Both Backs

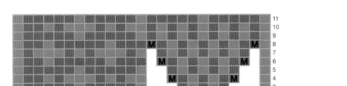

Right Palm

THUMB CHART

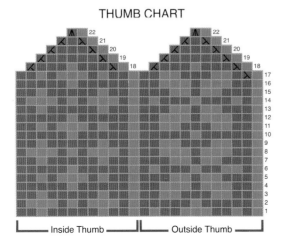

Inside Thumb — Outside Thumb

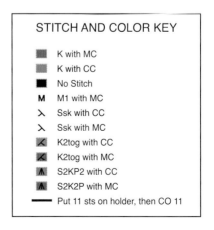

STITCH AND COLOR KEY

▨	K with MC
▨	K with CC
■	No Stitch
M	M1 with MC
⅄	Ssk with CC
⅄	Ssk with MC
⅄	K2tog with CC
⅄	K2tog with MC
⋀	S2KP2 with CC
⋀	S2K2P with MC
▬	Put 11 sts on holder, then CO 11

"MITTEN DAY" MITTENS

The tradition of unpacking the family mittens on October 14 dates back to the Middle Ages, when time was tracked using a wooden calendar stick. Since Sue's birthday is also October 14, we wanted to design a special set of mittens that anyone would be proud to unpack for the upcoming winter months.

The inspiration for the mittens was two contrasting pairs of red-and-black mittens that were made in the 1930s for a boy and a girl. Elements of both pairs were used in creating the updated version—the snowflake from the boy's mittens and the palm pattern from the girl's mittens. Also, the girl's mittens traditionally featured a lace pattern in the cuff while the boy's mittens used k1, p1 ribbing. To make the set more interesting, they are worked in positive and negative by reversing the main color and the contrasting color. The original mittens had characters on the thumbs, and we thought they were a nice touch, so we worked them into this pattern as well. It is interesting to note that the boy motif is upside down on the original mittens, while the girl's is right side up. The originals were donated to Vesterheim by Helga Lund Algyer in 1972.

SIZE
Child's average

Finished Measurements

Circumference: 7½"/19cm

Length: 9"/23cm

MATERIALS 3
Blackberry Ridge *Mer-Made DK Weight* (100% superwash merino wool, 114g/4oz, 260yds/238m per skein) Girl's version: 1 skein each Cream (MC) and Black (CC); Boy's version: 1 skein each Black (MC) and Cream (CC)

Size 4 (3.5mm) double-pointed needles (set of 5) or size needed to obtain gauge

Stitch markers, 1 in CC for beg of rnd

Tapestry needle

GAUGE
24 sts and 30 rnds = 4" (10cm) in stranded 2-color St st.

Adjust needle size as necessary to obtain correct gauge.

Pattern Notes

After working the cuff, follow the appropriate charts throughout and shape as indicated.

The colorwork is done using the "stranded" method, carrying both colors at once. Avoid long floats on the inside of the mitten in those areas where more than 5 consecutive stitches are worked in one color by catching the color not in use with the working color.

The directions are written for both the girl's and boy's versions of the mittens. Note that the cuffs, small charts, and thumbs are different for each version. The main mitten is the same for either version, but the background and contrasting colors are reversed.

The main chart shows the left-hand mitten; to make a right-hand mitten, mark the thumb gusset before working the palm pattern in the Setup Rnd, then work the Right Palm Chart.

Instructions
Left Mitten

Cuff

With dpns and MC, CO 40 sts; place marker and join, taking care not to twist sts.

Girl's version

Rnd 1: *K1, yo, S2KP2, k3, yo; rep from * around.

Rnd 2: Knit.

Rep Rnds 1 and 2 in the following stripe pattern: 6 total rnds MC, 1 rnd CC, 2 rnds MC, 2 rnds CC, 2 rnds MC, 1 rnd CC, 6 rnds MC.

Boy's version

Rnds 1–20: Work 20 rnds of k1, p1 Rib in the same stripe pattern as the girl's version.

Both versions

Work 9-rnd Cuff Chart (different for each version).

Thumb Gusset

Setup rnd: With MC, k34, pm, k5, pm, k1.

Join CC and follow Left Mitten Chart.

Rnds 3, 5, 7 (inc): Following chart, knit to gusset marker, slip marker, M1, knit to marker, M1, slip marker, k1—11 gusset sts between markers after last inc rnd.

Rnd 8: Knit to marker, remove markers, and slip 11 sts between markers to waste yarn or holder; CO 11 sts in pat to create thumb opening—46 sts.

Main Mitten

Work even following chart through Rnd 36, and on last rnd, pm between back hand and palm sts.

Top Mitten

Dec rnd: Cont to follow chart; *k1, ssk, knit to 2 sts before marker, k2tog; rep from * once more—42 sts.

Cont to follow chart and rep Dec rnd [every rnd] 9 times—8 sts.

Next Rnd: [K1, S2KP2] twice—4 sts.

Break yarn, leaving 6" tails.

With tapestry needle, thread yarn through rem sts, and pull tight; secure tails on WS.

Thumb

Slip 11 thumb gusset sts back to needle; with MC, pick up and knit 13 sts around the rem thumb opening—24 sts.

Attach CC; follow Thumb Chart for either girl's or boy's version through Rnd 12 and on last rnd, pm between front and back thumb sections.

Dec rnd: Cont to follow Thumb Chart; *k1, ssk, knit to 2 sts before marker, k2tog; rep from * once more—20 sts.

Cont to follow chart and work Dec rnd [every rnd] 3 times—8 sts.

Next Rnd: [K1, S2KP2] twice—4 sts.

Break yarn leaving 6" tails.

With tapestry needle, thread yarn through rem sts, and pull tight; secure tails on WS.

Right Mitten

Work cuff as for Left Mitten.

Thumb Gusset

Setup rnd: With MC, k24, pm, k5, pm, k11.

Work as for Left Mitten but follow Right Palm Chart for thumb gusset.

When finished with thumb gusset, complete as for Left Mitten.

Finishing

Weave in tails. Block.

LEFT MITTEN

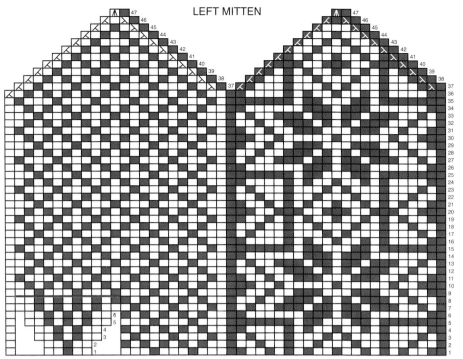

Left Palm Chart

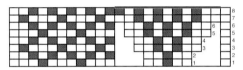

Right Palm Chart

STITCH AND COLOR KEY

- ☐ K with MC (see Note)
- ■ K with CC (see Note)
- ☐ No Stitch
- ⊟ Purl
- Ⓜ M1
- ⊠ Ssk
- ⊠ K2tog
- ⚠ S2KP2
- ── Put 11 sts on holder, then CO 11 in pattern

Note: Main Mitten and Palm Charts are the same for both versions, and are shown with Girl's version of MC/CC; reverse MC/CC for Boy's version.

Thumb and Cuff charts different for each version and are shown with correct MC/CC for version being worked.

THUMB CHART (Girl's)

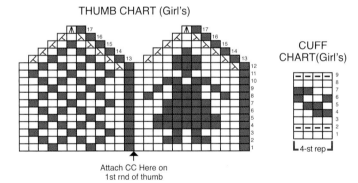

Attach CC Here on
1st rnd of thumb

CUFF CHART (Girl's)

└ 4-st rep ┘

THUMB CHART (Boy's)
(shown in Boy's MC/CC)

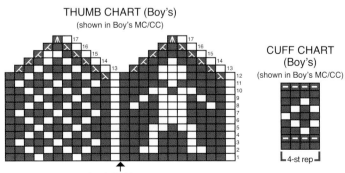

Attach CC Here on
1st rnd of thumb

CUFF CHART (Boy's)
(shown in Boy's MC/CC)

└ 4-st rep ┘

VOSS FAMILY SWEATERS

The two-color stranded ski sweater that we typically think of as traditional Norwegian knitting is a relatively recent addition to the textile heritage of Norway. Depending upon the region, color-knit garments did not come into fashion until the mid- to late-1800s. This sweater design was inspired by the Voss headscarf, which was discovered in an old immigrant's trunk that was packed away in a farmhouse attic. We also took note of and incorporated the tradition of making the background of a man's sweater dark with a light-colored foreground. The woman's is the opposite, with a light background and dark foreground.

SIZE(S)
Adult's X-small (small, medium, large, X-large, XX-large)

Instructions are given for smallest size, with larger sizes in parentheses. When only 1 number is given, it applies to all sizes.

FINISHED MEASUREMENTS
Chest: 38¾ (42, 45¼, 48½, 51½, 54¾)"/98 (107, 115, 123, 131, 139)cm

Body Length: 25¼ (26¾, 27¼, 28¼, 28¾, 29¼)"/64 (68, 69, 72, 73, 74)cm

Sleeve Length to Underarm: 19½ (19½, 20½, 20½, 21½)"/50 (50, 52, 52, 55)

MATERIALS ⬡3⬡
Cascade Yarns 220 (100% wool, 100g/3.5oz, 220yds/201m per skein)

Man's version: 3 (4, 4, 5, 5, 6) skeins Brown #7822 (MC), 3 (3, 4, 4, 5, 5) skeins Green Heather #9460 (A), and 1 skein Forest #9429 (B)

Woman's version: 3 (4, 4, 5, 5, 6) skeins Green Heather #9460 (MC), 3 (3, 4, 4, 5, 5) skeins Brown #7822 (A), and 1 skein Plum #7807 (B)

Size 5 (3.75mm) double-pointed needles (set of 5), 16"/40.5cm and 24"/61cm circular needles

Size 7 (4.5mm) double-pointed needles (set of 5) and 24"/61cm circular needles or size needed to obtain gauge

Tapestry needle

Cotton waste yarn

Stitch markers, 1 in CC for beg of rnd

GAUGE
20 sts and 24 rnds = 4" (10cm) in stranded 2-color St st.

Adjust needle size as necessary to obtain correct gauge.

Pattern Stitch
Corrugated Ribbing (multiple of 4 sts)

Rnd 1: *K2 MC, p2 B; rep from * around.

Rep Rnd 1 for pat.

Special Techniques
3-Needle Bind-Off: With RS tog and needles parallel, using a 3rd needle, knit tog a st from the front needle with 1 from the back. *Knit tog a st from the front and back needles, and sl the first st over the 2nd to bind off. Rep from * across, then fasten off last st.

Sewing and Cutting Steeks: See instructions on page 184.

Pattern Notes

The body of the sweater is worked in the round from the bottom up. After knitting, the armhole positions are marked, reinforced by machine sewing, then cut. This is called "steeking" (see page 184).

The neck opening is also formed using a sew-and-cut method.

The Body Chart shows only the right half of the body front; the left half is worked as a mirror image of the charted pattern. Note that the center stitch of the front, shown on the chart at the left edge and bordered in red, should *not* be repeated when repeating the pattern for the left half of the front. After working the mirror image for the left side, repeat the chart for both halves of the back.

The Sleeve Chart shows only the right half of the sleeve; the left half is worked as a mirror image of the charted pattern. The center stitch of the sleeve, shown on the chart at the left edge and bordered in red, should *not* be repeated when repeating the pattern for the left half of the sleeve.

The sweater includes an optional diamond pattern in the lower right corner. There are some design options provided, or you can design your personal design, such as initials, using the blank diamond outline provided. Substitute Diamond Chart for Body Chart in area where you desire to place diamond.

When working sleeve, switch to 16" circular needle when there are enough stitches to do so.

Instructions

Body

With smaller circular needle and B, CO 180 (192, 204, 216, 232, 244) sts; pm for beg of rnd and join, taking care not to twist sts.

Join A and work 2" in corrugated ribbing. Break B.

Inc rnd: Change to larger needle, join MC, and knit, increasing 14 (18, 22, 26, 26, 30) sts evenly around—194 (210, 226, 242, 258, 274) sts.

Next rnd: Knit with MC.

Next rnd (beg Band pat): *Beg at point designated for the size you are working, work 97 (105, 113, 121, 129, 137) sts in stranded 2-color St st across Rnd 1 of Band Chart, pm for side edge; rep from * for back.

Complete 29-rnd Band Chart.

Work Body Chart, beginning at the st and rnd indicated on chart for size you are working.

Place sts (including side st markers) on waste yarn to hold for sewing armholes and neck opening.

Sleeve

With smaller dpns and B, CO 40 (40, 44, 48, 52, 52) sts, pm for beg of rnd and join, taking care not to twist sts.

Join A and work 2" in corrugated ribbing. Break B.

Inc rnd: Change to larger dpns, join MC, and knit, increasing 11 (13, 13, 15, 15, 17) sts evenly around—51 (53, 57, 63, 67, 69) sts.

Next rnd: Knit with MC.

Work Rnds 1–4 of Sleeve Chart, beg where indicated for size being worked.

Inc rnd: Cont in established pat, k1, M1, knit to end of rnd, M1—53 (55, 59, 65, 69, 71) sts.

Cont working Sleeve Chart and rep Inc rnd [every 4 rnds] 21 (22, 23, 24, 24, 24) times more—95 (99, 105, 113 117, 119) sts.

Work even until sleeve measures 19½ (19½, 20½, 20½, 21½)" or desired length.

Facing

Beg working back and forth in rev St st with MC. (*See Alphabet sidebar on page 53 for directions on placing a secret message in the facing.*)

Row 1 (RS): Purl.

Row 2: K1, M1, knit to last st, M1, k1—97 (101, 107, 115, 119, 121) sts.

Row 3: P1, M1, purl to last st, M1, p1—99 (103, 109, 117, 121, 123) sts.

Rep [Rows 2 and 3] twice more—107 (111, 117, 125, 129, 131) sts.

Place sts on waste yarn for holder.

Weave in ends.

Block to finished measurements.

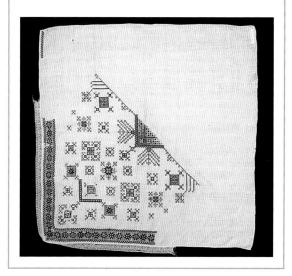

INSPIRED BY

This *skaut*, or headscarf, was probably made and worn by Ingeborg Larsdatter Lillethun of Vossestrand, Norway. Ingeborg immigrated in 1891 to Boone County, Illinois. She died in 1909.

Cut Armholes

Mark armhole depth below markers indicating sides of body. Using a contrasting piece of cotton yarn, baste a line from side marker to marked armhole depth position, going between 2 center side edge sts. (*See Marking, Sewing, and Cutting a Steek on page 184*).

After sewing in sleeves, loosely sew live sts of facing to WS of armhole, covering cut edge.

Neckline Mark And Sew

On front of sweater, mark off 31 (33, 37, 40, 43, 45) sts on each side of neck for shoulders. Slip rem 35 (39, 39, 41, 43, 47) sts to separate holder for neck. Mark neck depth of 3 (3, 3½, 3½, 3½, 4)" at center front. Using a piece of cotton yarn, baste the shape of neckline around front of sweater. With machine, sew along the marked neck 2 times and cut out crescent, leaving ¾" seam allowance.

Shoulder Join

Join shoulder seams using 3-needle BO.

Neck Edging

With smaller 16" circular needle, pick up and knit 112 (112, 116, 116, 116, 120) sts around neck as follows: *2A, 2B; rep from * around.

Work 7 rnds in corrugated rib. Break A.

Facing

Rnd 1: With B, knit.

Rnd 2: Purl.

Rnds 3–8: *K2, p2; rep from * around.

Fold facing to WS and secure by loosely sewing live sts to pickup rnd on the inside.

Finishing

Weave in all ends.

Block to finished measurements.

ADULT VOSS HALF-SLEEVE CHART

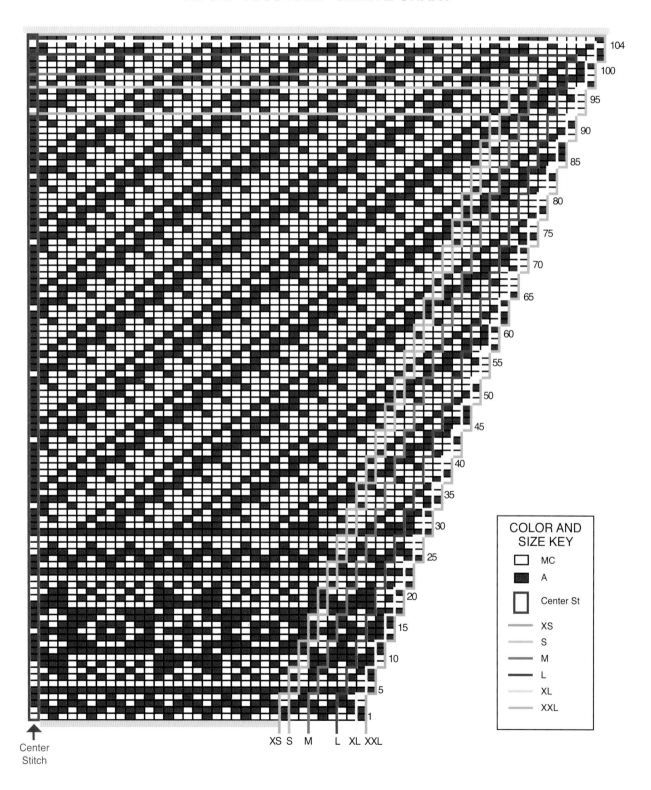

COLOR AND SIZE KEY

☐	MC
■	A
☐	Center St
——	XS
——	S
——	M
——	L
······	XL
——	XXL

Center Stitch

XS S   M   L   XL XXL

ADULT VOSS HALF-BODY CHART

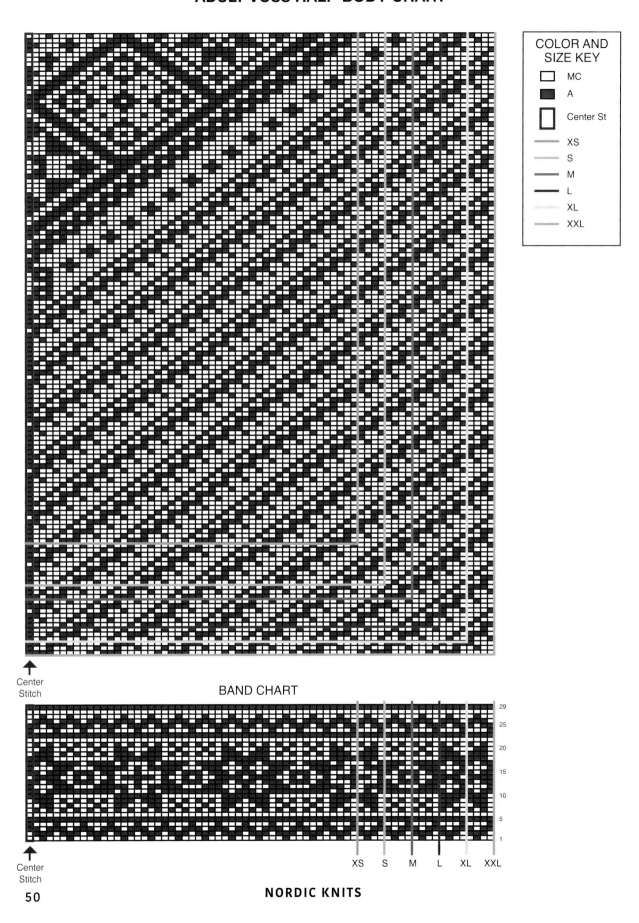

COLOR AND SIZE KEY

- ☐ MC
- ■ A
- ☐ Center St
- ─── XS
- ─── S
- ─── M
- ─── L
- ─── XL
- ─── XXL

↑
Center
Stitch

BAND CHART

29
25
20
15
10
5
1

↑
Center
Stitch

XS S M L XL XXL

FAMILY VOSS: OPTIONAL DIAMOND INSETS

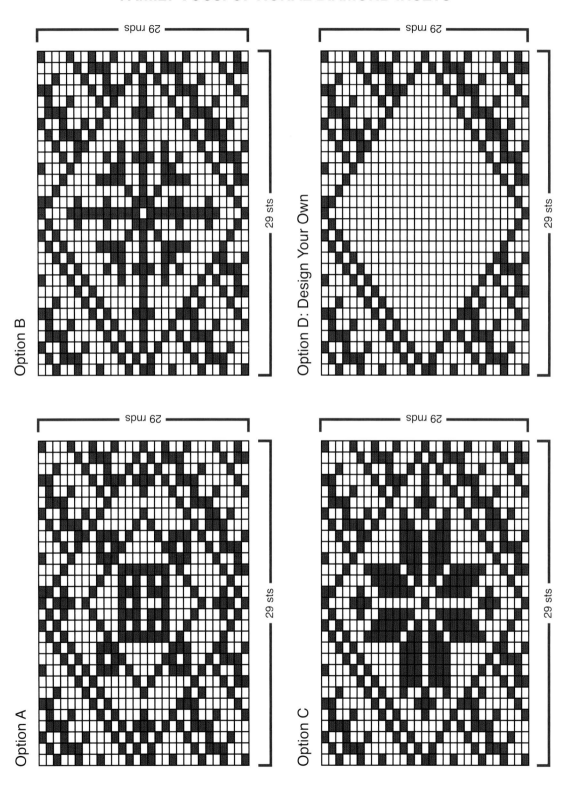

FAMILY VOSS SWEATER SCHEMATIC

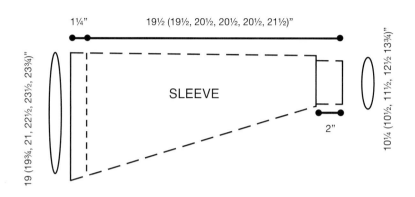

SLEEVE

1¼"

19½ (19½, 20½, 20½, 20½, 21½)"

19 (19¾, 21, 22½, 23½, 23¾)"

10¼ (10½, 11½, 12½ 13¾)"

2"

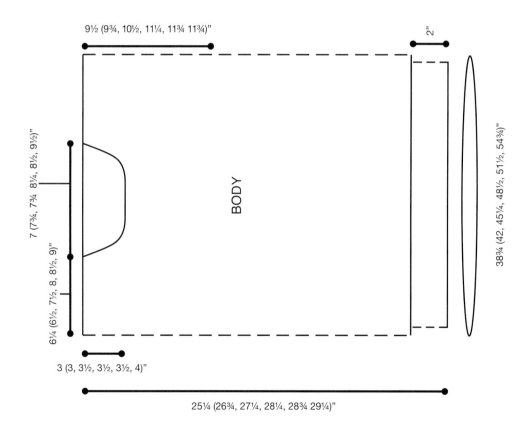

BODY

9½ (9¾, 10½, 11¼, 11¾ 11¾)"

2"

7 (7¾, 7¾ 8¼, 8½, 9½)"

6¼ (6½, 7½, 8, 8½, 9)"

3 (3, 3½, 3½, 3½, 4)"

38¾ (42, 45¼, 48½, 51½, 54¾)"

25¼ (26¾, 27¼, 28¼, 28¾ 29¼)"

ALPHABET SLEEVE FACING CHART

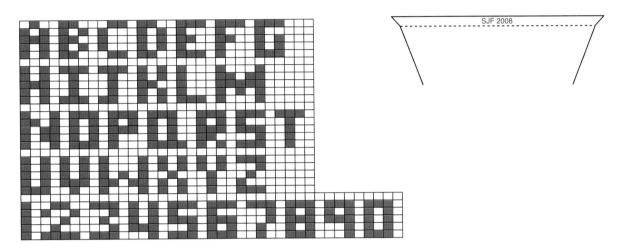

Step 1: Chart out message on graph paper.

Step 2: Determine the center of the message and mark off the desired number of sts needed to center the message in the facing sts.

Step 3: Work facing in reverse St st making sure that the first row is plain (not two-color). After completing the first row, add charted message to the next five rows. Knit final row in background color and thread sts onto yarn holder for sewing inside sleeve.

KIDS' VOSS SWEATERS

These kids' sweaters are a simplified version of the heavily-patterned adult sweater. This is a perfect set to make and wear as a family.

SIZES
Child's small (medium, large, X-large)

Instructions are given for smallest size, with larger sizes in parentheses. When only 1 number is given, it applies to all sizes.

FINISHED MEASUREMENTS
Chest: 26 (27½, 30, 31½)"/66 (70, 76, 80)cm

Body Length: 17 (19, 21, 23)"/43 (48, 53, 58)cm

Sleeve Length to Underarm: 11 (13, 15, 16)"/28 (33, 38, 41)cm

MATERIALS 3
Cascade Yarns 220 (100% wool, 100g/3.5oz, 220yds/201m per skein)

Girl's version: 3 skeins Red #9404 (MC) and 1 skein each White #8505 (A) and Blue #7818 (B)

Boy's version: 3 skeins Blue #7817 (MC) and 1 skein each White #8505 (A) and Red #9404 (B)

Size 5 (3.75mm) double-pointed needles (set of 5), 16"/40.5cm and 24"/61cm circular needles

Size 7 (4.5mm) double-pointed needles (set of 5) and 24"/61cm circular needles or size needed to obtain gauge

Stitch markers, 1 in CC for beg of rnd

Tapestry needle

Cotton waste yarn for steeking

Sewing machine

GAUGE
20 sts and 24 rnds = 4" (10cm) in stranded 2-color St st with larger needles.

Adjust needle size as necessary to obtain correct gauge.

Pattern Stitch
Corrugated Ribbing (multiple of 4 sts)

Rnd 1: *K2 MC, p2 B; rep from * around.

Rep Rnd 1 for pat.

Special Technique
3-Needle Bind-Off: With RS tog and needles parallel, using a 3rd needle, knit tog a st from the front needle with 1 from the back. *Knit tog a st from the front and back needles, and slip the first st over the 2nd to bind off. Rep from * across, then fasten off last st.

Pattern Notes
The body of the sweater is worked in the round from the bottom up. After knitting, the armhole positions are marked, reinforced by machine sewing, then cut. This is called "steeking" (see page 184).

The neck opening is also formed using a sew-and-cut method.

The red version of the sweater includes a "lice pattern" on the body and sleeve of the sweater, as shown in the chart. Omit the lice pattern for the blue version; work in solid color.

When working sleeve, switch to 16" circular needle when there are enough stitches to do so.

Instructions

Body

With smaller needle and B, CO 124 (132, 140, 148) sts; pm for beg of rnd and join, taking care not to twist sts.

Rnds 1–14: Join A and work in corrugated ribbing. Break B.

Inc rnd: Change to larger needle, join MC, and knit, increasing 6 (6, 10, 10) sts evenly around—130 (138, 150, 158) sts.

Preparation rnd: With MC, k65 (69, 75, 79), pm for side edge, k65 (69, 75, 79).

Work Kids' Chart; *beg where indicated for size being worked and working 32-st rep twice, then work to end point for size being worked, slip marker; rep from * for back.

Cont working charted pat as established through Rnd 27.

Red version only: Rep 12-rnd lice pat until piece measures approx 14 (16, 18, 20)", ending with 3 rnds MC.

Blue version only: Work even in MC only until piece measures 14 (16, 18, 20)".

Both versions: Work 15-rnd Shoulder pat, completing chart.

Place sts (including side st markers) on waste yarn to hold for sewing armholes and neck opening.

Sleeve

With smaller dpns and B, CO 36 (36, 40, 40) sts; pm for beg of rnd and join, taking care not to twist sts.

Join A and work 2" in corrugated ribbing. Break B.

Inc rnd: Change to larger needle, join MC, and knit, increasing 4 (4, 6, 6) sts evenly around—40 (40, 46, 46) sts.

Next rnd: Knit with MC.

Work 15-rnd Shoulder pat, then work 12-rnd lice pat (Red version) or solid MC (Blue version); *at the same time,* work Inc rnd [every 3 rnds] 6 (12, 0, 2) times, then [every 4 rnds] 9 (6, 18, 18) times, working new sts into established pat, as follows:

Inc rnd: K1, M1, knit to end of rnd, M1—70 (76, 82, 86) sts when inc rnds are complete.

Work even until sleeve measures 11 (13, 15, 16) " or desired length.

Facing

Beg working back and forth in rev St st with MC. (*See alphabet chart sidebar on page 53 for directions on placing a secret message in the facing.*)

Row 1 (RS): Purl.

Row 2: K1, M1, knit to last st, M1, k1—72 (78, 84, 88) sts.

INSPIRED BY
Detail of Voss headscarf.

Row 3: P1, M1, purl to last st, M1, p1—74 (80, 86, 90) sts.

Rep Rows 2 and 3 twice more—82 (88, 94, 98) sts.

Place sts on waste yarn for holder.

Finishing

Weave in ends. Block to finished measurements.

Cut Armholes

Mark armhole depth below markers indicating sides of body. Using a contrasting piece of cotton yarn, baste a line from side marker to marked armhole depth position, going between 2 side edge sts. (*See page 184.*) After sewing in sleeves, loosely sew live sts of facing to WS of armhole, covering cut edge.

Neckline Mark and Sew

On front of sweater, mark off 19 (20, 22, 24) sts on each side of neck for shoulders. Slip rem 27 (29, 31, 31) sts to separate holder for neck. Mark neck depth 3" down from center front neck. Using a piece of cotton yarn, baste the shape of neckline around front of sweater. With machine, sew along the marked neck 2 times. Cut out crescent, leaving ¾" seam allowance from sewn line.

Shoulder Join

Join shoulder seams using 3-needle BO.

Neck Edging

With smaller 16" circular needle, pick up and knit 76 (76, 80, 80) sts around neck as follows: *2A, 2B, rep from * around.

Work 6 rnds in corrugated rib. Break A.

Facing
Rnd 1: With B, knit.

Rnd 2: Purl.

Rnds 3–8: *K2, p2; rep from * around.

Fold facing inside neckline and secure by loosely sewing live sts to pickup rnd on the inside.

KIDS' VOSS SWEATER CHART

COLOR KEY
- ☐ MC
- ■ CC

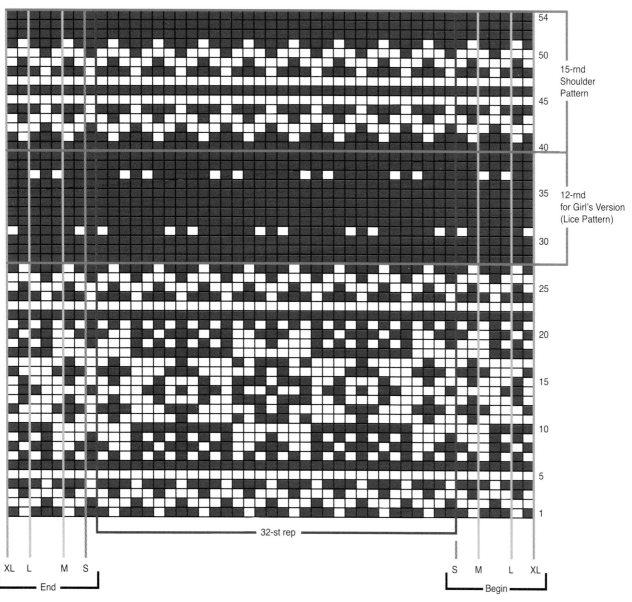

15-rnd
Shoulder
Pattern

12-rnd
for Girl's Version
(Lice Pattern)

54
50
45
40
35
30
25
20
15
10
5
1

32-st rep

XL L M S
End

S M L XL
Begin

VOSS SELF-FRINGING SHAWL

In addition to providing inspiration for the Voss Family Sweaters, the cross-stitch motifs in the embroidered headscarf were used to create the Voss Self-Fringing Shawl.

The design along the edge of the shawl uses six different diamond patterns drawn from the original piece. The inner pattern on the shawl is called the Tree of Life and appears to grow from the center out. It is interesting to note that this main pattern consists of a simple two-row repeat that is shifted over every other row to create the branchlike appearance of the "tree."

FINISHED MEASUREMENTS
Width along top of shawl: 66"/168cm

Length down center of shawl: 32"/81cm

MATERIALS 🧶3
Blackberry Ridge *Mer-Made DK Wool* (100% superwash merino wool, 114g/4oz, 260yds/238m skein): 3 skeins Black (MC) and 2 skeins Natural Cream (CC)

Size 5 (3.75mm) 30"/76cm circular needle

Size 7 (4.5mm) 30"/76cm circular needle or size needed to obtain gauge

Tapestry needle

GAUGE
24 sts and 27 rows = 4" (10cm) in stranded 2-color St st with larger needle.

Adjust needle size as necessary to obtain correct gauge.

Pattern Notes

The shawl is self-fringing and is worked with the right side facing you on every row. Attach and break the yarn at the beginning and end of each row, leaving 6" tails at both ends. After completing two rows, tie the four yarn tails together with an overhand knot to make fringe at both edges of the shawl.

The charted pattern shows only the right half of the shawl. The other half of the shawl is worked as a mirror image of the charted pattern. The center stitch of the shawl, shown on the chart at the left edge and bordered in red, should *not* be repeated when repeating the pattern for the left half of the shawl.

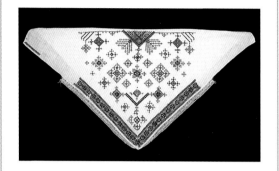

Instructions

With larger needle and MC, leaving a 6" tail, CO 3 sts; break yarn, leaving a 6" tail.

Start from right edge of knitting and work chart.

Row 1: Attach MC, leaving a 6" tail; k1f&b, k1, k1f&b; break yarn, leaving a 6" tail—5 sts.

Row 2: Attach both MC and CC, leaving a 6" tail; k1f&b, k3 following chart, k1f&b; break both yarns, leaving 6" tails.

Continue working chart, increasing in the first and last st of each row, attaching new yarns at beg of each row and breaking them at end, leaving 6" tails, and tying 4 yarn tails together at each edge after completing 2 rows.

Complete 101-row chart once, then rep from A to B.

Facing

Change to smaller needle; work back and forth.

Rows 1 (RS) and 2: Knit with MC.

Row 3: K1, ssk, knit to last 3 sts, k2tog, k1.

Row 4: P1, p2tog, purl to last 3 sts, ssp, p1.

Rep [Rows 3 and 4] twice more.

BO very loosely with larger needle in right hand.

Block shawl and facing.

Fold facing and sew to WS; keep sts loose (do not pull too tight) to maintain the elasticity of the fabric.

VOSS SHAWL CHART

KEY

- ▨ MC
- ☐ CC
- ▯ Center Stitch
- — A/B--Rep between these lines

ENTRELAC WRISTERS

The only piece of entrelac knitting at Vesterheim is a pair of knee-length red-and-black entrelac socks. The socks, which belonged to Jensine Nelson Hansen of Vefsen, Norway, were brought to Wisconsin in 1889 and donated to the museum in 1971. Because the socks use a technique rarely seen in Norwegian knitting, the socks are featured in the knitting display in the museum.

The entrelac or "basket-weave" technique is most commonly recognized as a Finnish knitting technique. Entrelac is fun to learn. Although it appears as if the squares are sewn together, the squares are actually joined to each other as they are knit. With each completed square comes a feeling of satisfaction and the anticipation of moving on to the next square.

FINISHED MEASUREMENTS
Circumference: 7"/18cm

Width: 5½"/14cm

MATERIALS ⬡3⬡
Dale of Norway *Heilo* (100% wool, 50g/1.75oz, 109yds/100m per ball): 1 ball each Tartan Green #7562 (A), Moss Green #9335 (B), Sand Heather #0004 (C), and Grey Heather #0007 (D)

Size 4 (3.5mm) double-pointed needles (set of 5) or 11"/28cm circular needles or size needed to obtain gauge

GAUGE
24 sts and 30 rows = 4" (10cm) in St st.

Adjust needle size as necessary to obtain correct gauge.

Special Abbreviations

(See Knitting from Left to Right instructions on page 184)

KLR: Knit from left to right

WB: Work back

Pattern Stitch

Garter Chevron (multiple of 12 sts)

Rnd 1: *K1, yo, k4, S2KP2, k4, yo; rep from * around.

Rnd 2: Purl.

Rep Rnds 1 and 2 for pat.

Pattern Notes

The wrister begins with a garter stitch chevron pattern that fits into the square entrelac pattern.

If using double-pointed needles, you may need to shift the stitches from one needle to another during the entrelac section.

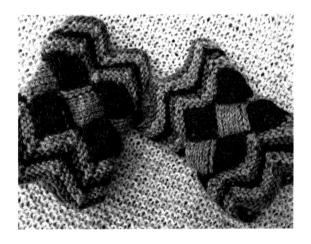

Instructions

Step 1: Garter Chevron

Using long-tail method and A, CO 48 sts; pm for beg of rnd and join, taking care not to twist sts.

Purl 1 rnd.

Work Garter Chevron pat in following stripe sequence: 2 rnds each B, C, D, A, B, C.

Step 2: First Set of Squares (Left-Leaning)

With D, mark into sets of 12 sts and work four squares.

First Square (Left-Leaning) *See Figure 1.*

Row 1: K6.

Row 2: (WB) Sl 1, KLR5.

Row 3: Sl 1, k4, k2tog-tbl (1 st in D and 1 in C).

Rep [Rows 2 and 3] 5 more times. Square complete.

Rep around to make 4 left-leaning squares with D.

First round of squares complete. Break D.

Step 3: Second Set of Squares (Right-Leaning)

With C, work 4 right-leaning squares.

With RH needle, pick up 6 loops (without knitting them) along slip-st edge of first square, then attach C at tip of square and begin knitting backward.

Row 1: (WB) KLR6, turn. *See Figure 2.*

Row 2: Sl 1, k5, turn.

Row 3: (WB) Sl 1, KLR4, KLR2tog, Turn.

NOTE: *This joins the newly forming square to the sts of the last square worked on previous round.*

Rep [Rows 2 and 3] 5 more times. Square complete.

Rep around to make 4 right-leaning squares with C. 2nd round of squares complete. Break C.

Step 4: Third Set of Squares (Left-Leaning)

With LH needle, pick up 6 loops (without knitting them) along slip-st edge of first square, then attach D at tip of square and begin knitting forward.

Complete square following Step 2.

Rep for rem 3 squares. Break D.

Step 5: Garter Chevron

Rnd 1: With C, working from right to left, *k6 live sts of next square, pick up and knit 6 sts along slip-st edge; rep from * around, pm for beg of rnd—48 sts.

Rnd 2: Purl.

Work Garter Chevron pat in following stripe sequence: 2 rnds each B, A, D, C, B, C. On last (purl) rnd of C, bind off very loosely pwise.

Finishing

Weave in ends. Block to finished measurements.

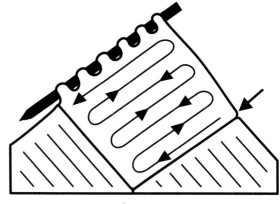

Figure 1

Figure 2

INSPIRED BY

These socks belonged to Jensine Nelson Hansen (b. 1872) of Vefsen, Norway, and were brought to Wisconsin in 1889.

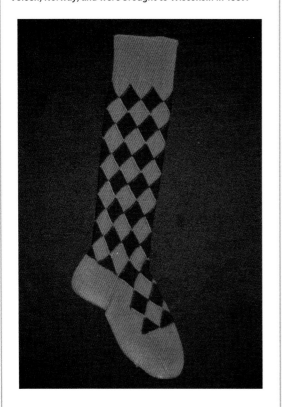

VIKING PILLOW

The focal point of the Viking Pillow was drawn from the tapestry weaving shown with this project that depicts three ships on the ocean framed by a border of birds and maidens.

FINISHED MEASUREMENTS
14 x 14"/36 x 36cm

MATERIALS 4
Cascade Yarns 220 (100% wool, 100g/3.5oz, 220yds/201m skein): 2 skeins each Blue #7818 (MC) and White #8505 (CC); 1 skein Red #9404 (A)

Size 7 (4.5mm) 24"/61cm double-pointed needles (set of 2) and circular needles or size needed to obtain gauge

Medium-size crochet hook

Stitch markers, 1 in CC for beg of rnd

14"/36cm square pillow form

Tapestry needle

GAUGE
20 sts and 26 rnds = 4" (10cm) in stranded 2-color St st.

Adjust needle size as necessary to obtain correct gauge.

Special Techniques
Provisional Cast-On: With crochet hook and waste yarn, make a chain several sts longer than desired cast-on. With knitting needle and project yarn, pick up indicated number of sts in the "bumps" on back of chain. When indicated in pattern, "unzip" the crochet chain to free live sts.

Applied Twisted I-Cord Edging: See page 66.

Pattern Notes
The pillow is worked in the round.

The chart is knit with MC and CC only; the small red sections are duplicate-stitched after pillow is complete.

I-cord edging is applied after the pillow has been stuffed and sewn together. Directions are given for the applied twisted I-cord, which is attached as it is knit. If you must, the I-cord can be knit separately and then sewn on, but the applied technique is preferred.

Instructions

Using provisional method and MC, CO 136 sts; place marker and join, taking care not to twist sts.

Follow chart, repeating the Viking ship motif twice around the pillow and working "red" stitches in white (CC).

Continue until 77-rnd chart is complete.

Slip sts of 2nd rep of chart to a separate needle and graft top front and back sts of pillow tog using Kitchener st.

With tapestry needle and A, work the red stitches using duplicate st.

Finishing

Weave in ends and block pillow.

Stuff with pillow form.

Unzip provisional cast-on, slipping front and back sts to separate needles; graft bottom front and back sts tog using Kitchener st.

Follow Applied Twisted I-Cord instructions (see page 66) to complete edging.

INSPIRED BY

The tapestry that inspired the Viking Pillow was designed by the Norwegian painter Frederik Collet and woven by Aagot Lund from Ørje, Norway. It was purchased by the donor in Oslo in 1936. Luther College Collection.

Attaching and twisting I-cords.

Applied Twisted I-cord

This I-cord is attached to the edges of the pillow as it is knit; there's no need to sew it on afterward. Two separate I-cords are worked simultaneously, each twisted around the other, then attached to the main pillow fabric. Five-inch double-pointed needles are the perfect tools for working this technique. One I-cord is worked with MC, the other with CC.

Unattached I-cord: With dpns, CO 3 sts. K3, *do not turn work, place RH needle in left hand and slip sts to other end of dpn, wrap yarn around back of work and k3 Rnd 1: *K3, do not turn work, place RH needle in left hand and slip sts to other end of dpn, wrap yarn around back of work, ready to knit; rep from * until cord is desired length; rep Rnd 1 as indicated in pattern.

Mark every 3rd st around all 4 edges of the pillow. Starting at lower corner, *work 3 rnds of unattached I-cord with MC, and after last rnd, pick up (but do not knit) 1 marked st from pillow edge and place on left end of LH needle.

Next rnd: K2, k2tog-tbl (attaching MC I-cord to pillow edge). Work 8 rnds of unattached I-cord with MC. Start 2nd I-cord with CC. Work 3 rnds of unattached I-cord, then pick up the next marked st from the pillow edge and place on left end of LH needle.

Next rnd: K2, k2tog-tbl (attaching CC I-cord to pillow edge). Work 8 rnds of unattached I-cord with CC. Twist MC around CC and repeat from * around pillow.

VIKING SHIP PILLOW CHART

COLOR KEY
- ▨ Blue
- ☐ White
- ⊡ Knit with White, Duplicate St with Red

├─── 68-st rep ───┤

SWEDISH
HANDKNITS

Influenced by the variety of knitting techniques and styles found in Swedish textiles, the patterns here gather a number of these extensive knitting traditions all in one place.

In this collection of patterns, you will find elements of traditional immigrant items and Swedish American–made items, such as weavings, paintings, and other handwork, that served as inspiration.

There are regional knitting traditions such as the Swedish Mittens, made on the Island of Gotland, twined knitting from the Darlana area of Sweden, and the more famous Swedish knitting traditions of the Bohus knitting cooperative. In some cases, techniques were modified to honor knitters who have come before us, and in other cases, some new techniques are shown.

Although these designs are basic in nature, completing them provides the satisfaction of a hearty, useful item worthy of your time and a project well done. These items are examples of what a busy pioneer immigrant may have knit for their family after first attending to numerous other chores. Notice the use of color and the simple beauty in each of these items.

LONG STOCKING HAT

The colorful stained-glass window on the stairway landing at the American Swedish Institute is known as the Visby Window. The man in the center panel wears a beautiful long red stocking hat. Draped over his hand is the end of another wonderfully long red stocking hat, which offered the inspiration for this pattern. The hat appears to have some texture, but it was difficult to determine the exact pattern. We used a beautiful kettle-dyed red yarn that adds a more vintage feel to the hat and is reminiscent of the oil painting depicted in the Visby Window.

SIZE
Adult's average

FINISHED MEASUREMENTS
Circumference: 20"/51cm

Height: 45"/114.5cm (from top to tip)

MATERIALS 🧶4🧶
Ewetopia Fibers *Hand-Dyed Montana Merino* (100% wool, 8oz/280g, 560yds/550m): Kettle-dyed Holly Berry, 1 skein

Size 6 (4mm), 16"/40.5cm long circular and double-pointed needles (dpns) or size needed to obtain gauge

Stitch markers (one in CC for beg of rnd)

GAUGE
20 sts and 28 rows = 4"/10cm in St st.

Adjust needle size as necessary to obtain correct gauge.

Instructions

With MC and circular needle, CO 100 sts. Pm for beg of rnd and join, taking care not to twist sts.

Ribbing: Work around in k2, p2 rib for 2"/5cm.

Rnds 1–53: Foll chart.

Decreases

Place second marker after the 48th st.

Rnd 1: K1, p2, k2tog, k to 2 sts before marker, ssk, slm (slip marker), p2, k1, p2, k2tog, k to 2 sts before next marker, ssk (4 sts dec'd).

Rnds 2–12: Work in est pat.

Rep Dec Rnds 1–12 until 16 sts rem, ending after Rnd 12.

Last Dec Rnd: K1, p2, S2KP2, p2, k1, p2, S2KP2, p2—12 sts rem.

Work 11 more rnds as est, break yarn, leaving a 6"/15cm tail.

With tapestry needle, thread tail through rem sts, pull tight to close. Secure on WS.

Finishing

Weave in all ends. Block to finished measurements.

INSPIRED BY

The colorful stained-glass window on the stairway landing at the American Swedish Institute is known as the Visby Window. The man in the center panel wears a beautiful long red stocking hat which offered the inspiration for this pattern. The hat appears to have some texture, but it was difficult to determine the exact pattern.

LONG STOCKING HAT CHART

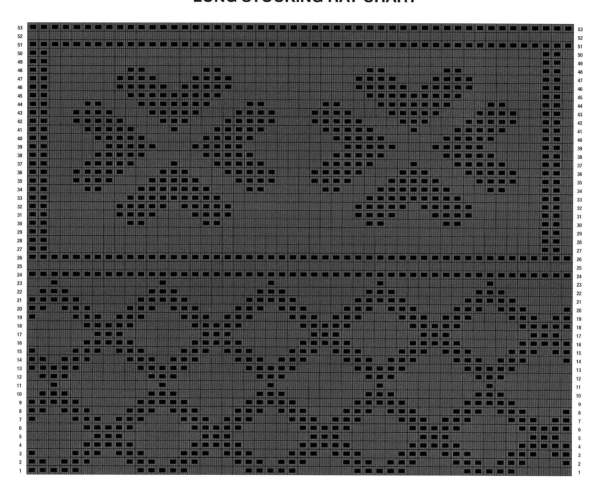

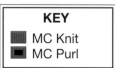

KEY

MC Knit
MC Purl

SAMI HAT, SCARF, AND GAUNTLET MITTENS

The Sami people, formerly known as Lapps or Laplanders, are indigenous to not only Sweden but Norway, Finland, and Russia as well. The Sami keep herds of reindeer for food, much as the Native Americans relied on buffalo. Despite the numerous physical, political, or economic hardships the Sami have experienced through the centuries, their handwork traditions remain strong and vital—a rallying point and source of cultural and artistic pride. We can imagine this hat, scarf, and mitten set being worn by the Sami people on one of their extremely cold and snowy days. The colors would brighten up even the darkest morning.

Swedish Handknits

SAMI HAT

SIZE
Adult's average

MATERIALS 4
Cascade Yarns *220* (100% wool, 100g/3.5oz, 220yds/201m): 1 skein in each Blue #9457 (MC), Cream #8010 (A), Yellow #7828 (B), Green #9490 (C), Red #8895 (D)

Size 7 (4.5mm), 16"/40.5cm long needle

Size 8 (5mm), 16"/40.5cm long needle or size needed to obtain gauge

Cotton waste yarn

Stitch marker

Tapestry needle

Pom-pom maker (optional)

GAUGE
20 sts and 24 rnds = 4"/10cm in solid color St st on larger needle.

Adjust needle size as necessary to obtain correct gauge.

NORDIC KNITS

Special Techniques

Crochet Cast-On (see Special Techniques Used, page 185)

Kitchener Stitch (see Special Techniques Used, page 185)

Instructions

Facing

Using Crochet Cast-On method and smaller needle, CO 96 sts. Pm for beg of rnd and join, taking care not to twist sts.

With MC, work around in St st for 5"/12.5cm.

Next Rnd (turning ridge): Purl.

Main Hat

Change to larger needle.

Foll Chart Rows 1–33, working around in St st.

Remove provisional CO and place live sts on smaller needle. Fold facing inside hat so that WS's are tog. *Holding the two needles parallel and using MC, knit the 1st st on the front needle and the 1st st on the back needle tog as 1 st; rep from * around until all sts of the facing are joined to the hat. At the end of this row, all the sts should be on the larger needle.

With MC, work around in St st for 4"/10cm.

Using Kitchener stitch, close top of hat.

Finishing

Weave in all ends. Block.

Pom-Poms (make 2)

Use pom-pom maker or follow instructions as follows:

Cut two cardboard circles the size of desired pom-pom. Cut a hole in the center of each circle, approx ½"/1.25cm in diameter. Thread a tapestry needle with one very long strand of MC, B, and D. Holding both circles together, insert needle through center hole, over the outside edge, and through center again, going around and around until entire circle is covered and center hole is filled (thread more lengths of yarn as needed). With sharp scissors, cut yarn between the

two circles all around the circumference. Using two 12"/30.5cm strands of yarn (tying ends), wrap yarn between circles, going two or three times around; pull tight and tie into a firm knot. Remove cardboard and fluff out the pom-pom. Trim ends as necessary to make pom-pom circular. Attach a pom-pom to each point on top of hat.

SAMI CHART

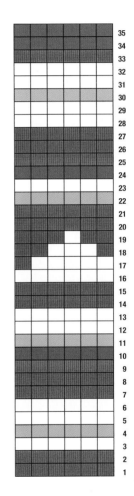

COLOR KEY

■	MC Knit
■	Color A Knit
□	Color B Knit
■	Color C Knit
□	Color D Knit

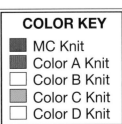

SAMI SCARF

FINISHED MEASUREMENTS
9"/23cm wide x 66"/167.5cm long

MATERIALS 4
Cascade Yarns 220 (100% wool,
100g/3.5oz, 220yds/201m): 4
skeins Blue #9457 (MC); 1 skein
each Cream #8010 (A), Yellow
#7828 (B), Green #9490 (C), Red
#8895 (D)

Size 8 (5mm), 16"/40.5cm long
circular needles or size needed
to obtain gauge (2)

Crochet hook size I-9 (5mm)

Cotton waste yarn

Tapestry needle

Stitch markers (2)

GAUGE
20 sts and 24 rnds = 4"/10cm
in solid color St st on larger
needle.

*Adjust needle size as necessary to
obtain correct gauge.*

Special Techniques
Provisional Cast-On (see Special Techniques Used, page 185)

Instructions
Scarf First Half
With waste yarn, and using the provisional method, CO 84 sts. Place first marker for beg of rnd and second marker after 42 sts to mark the center. Join, taking care not to twist sts.

Foll chart, working 33 rnds of colorwork.

Change to MC and work around in St st until 27"/68.5cm above last row of colorwork (center of scarf).

Turn piece inside out and weave in ends. Unravel provisional cast-on and, using Kitchener stitch, close the beg end tog.

Faux side seam: Remove first marker at beg of rnd. Drop the 1st st all the way down to the colorwork section and stop before it unravels into the colorwork. With crochet hook, slip st back up the "bars" created by dropping the st two at a time (if this were a dropped st you would pick up one "bar" at a time; however, to make this seam pronounced, you will be picking up two "bars" at a time, which will make the scarf lie flat to create a decorative effect).

Rep the dropped st in the same manner after the second marker. Keep sts on needle.

Scarf Second Half
Rep for second half using second needle and keeping the second half on your needle.

Finishing
Using Kitchener stitch, join the two halves tog.

Weave in all ends. Block to finished measurements.

INSPIRED BY
Set of wool felt Sami hats, American Swedish Institute Collection.

SAMI GAUNTLET MITTENS

SIZE
Adult's average

FINISHED MEASUREMENTS
Circumference at palm: 8"/20.5cm

Length: 14"/35cm

MATERIALS 🧶4🧶
Cascade Yarns *220* (100% wool, 100g/3.5oz, 220yds/201m): 2 skeins Blue #9457 (MC); 1 skein in each of Cream #8010 (A), Yellow #7828 (B), Green #9490 (C), Red #8895 (D)

Cascade Yarns *Eco Duo* (70% undyed baby alpaca/30% undyed merino wool, 100g/3.5oz, 197yds/180m): 1 skein Tan and Cream #1702 (E)

Size 8 (5mm) double-pointed needles or size needed to obtain gauge

Size 6 (4mm) double-pointed needles or two sizes smaller than size needed to obtain gauge

Size 7 (4.5mm), 16"/40.5cm long circular needle

Cotton waste yarn

Stitch markers (2)

Tapestry needle

GAUGE
20 sts and 24 rnds = 4"/10cm in solid color St st on larger needle.

Adjust needle size as necessary to obtain correct gauge.

Instructions (make 2)

Facing
Using waste yarn and provisional cast-on method, CO 48 sts. Pm for beg of rnd and join, taking care not to twist sts. Change to MC and divide sts evenly on larger dpns.

Rnd 1: Knit.

Rnd 2: Knit, inc 6 sts evenly spaced on rnd—54 sts.

Rnds 3–34: Knit.

Rnd 35: Purl for turning ridge.

Gauntlet
Rnds 36–67: Foll Chart Rows 1–32.

Rnd 68: Work Row 33 of chart, working k2tog evenly spaced across rnd six times—48 sts.

Rnds 69–71: Work last 3 rows of chart.

Remove provisional CO and place live sts on smaller needle. Fold facing inside of mitten so that WS's are tog. *Holding the two needles parallel and using MC, knit the 1st st on the front needle and the 1st st on the back needle tog as 1 st; rep from * around until all sts of the facing are joined to the gauntlet. At the end of this row, all the sts should be on the larger needle.

Change to smaller dpns and dec 8 sts evenly around—40 sts.

Ribbing
With MC, work in k1, p1 rib for 6 rnds.

Change to larger dpns.

Main Mitten
Rnd 1: Knit, inc 2 sts evenly spaced around—42 sts.

Rnds 2–4: Knit.

Thumb Gusset
Rnd 5: K20, pm, k1f&b, k1f&b, pm, k20—44 sts.

Rnd 6: Knit.

Rnd 7: K to marker, k1f&b, k to 1 st before marker, k1f&b, k to end of rnd.

Rep last 2 rnds until there are 16 sts between markers.

Hand
Next Rnd: Knit to marker, remove marker, k1, place next 14 sts on holder, k1, remove marker, k to end of rnd—42 sts.

Cont even until mitten length is even with height of pinky finger.

Top of Mitten
Rnd 1: (K4, k2tog) seven times around—35 sts.

Rnd 2: Knit.

Rnd 3: (K3, k2tog) seven times around—28 sts.

Rnd 4: Knit.

Rnd 5: (K2, k2tog) seven times around—21 sts.

Rnd 6: Knit.

Rnd 7: (K1, k2tog) seven times around—14 sts.

Rnd 8: Knit.

Rnd 9: (K2tog) seven times—7 sts.

Break yarn, leaving a 6"/15cm tail. Using tapestry needle, thread tail through rem sts, pull tight, and weave in end.

Thumb
Distributing sts evenly on 3 dpns, sl 14 thumb gusset sts to larger dpns; then, with MC, pick up and k2 sts at thumb opening, pm for beg of rnd—16 sts.

Work even in St st until thumb is 2 3/4"/7cm or until thumb height is even with thumb nail height.

Dec Rnd: (K2, k2tog) four times—12 sts.

Work 2 rnds even.

Dec Rnd: (K1, ktog) four times—8 sts.

Work 1 rnd even.

Dec Rnd: (K2tog) four times—4 sts.

Break yarn, leaving a 6"/15cm tail. Using tapestry needle, thread tail through rem sts, pull tight, and weave in end.

Mitten Lining

Turn mitten inside out. Using E, beg at the base of the mitten ribbing, pick up and k40 sts around.

Work lining as for mitten from ribbing directions to thumb directions.

Turn mittens right side out, making sure mitten lining lies smoothly inside mitten.

STAINED-GLASS HAT

The Swedish are known for their beautiful handmade glass. The American Swedish Institute's glass collection pays homage to this rich tradition by showcasing exquisite glass pieces that draw you in and beg to be looked at up close. Many of these pieces served as inspiration for the patterns in the Swedish Handknits section, including the Stained-Glass Hat. The color progression in Noro Kureyon makes knitting this hat an adventure. When we knit this hat, we could hardly wait to get to the next section of color to see how it would spill out of the skein. The color combinations reminded us of how melted glass blends together into mesmerizing fields of wonder. The hat is constructed employing a traditional modular knitting technique called "domino knitting." The squares that make up this hat show off the self-striping yarn perfectly.

SIZE
Adult's medium/large

FINISHED MEASUREMENTS
Circumference at head: 20"/51cm

Height: 10"/25.5cm

MATERIALS 4
Noro *Kureyon* (100% wool, 50g/1.75oz, 108yd/99m): 2 skeins Color #170

Size 8 (5mm), 16"/40.5cm long circular and double-pointed needles or size needed to obtain gauge

Stitch markers (5)

Tapestry needle

GAUGE
18 sts and 10 rows = 4"/10cm in Garter st.

20 sts and 28 rows = 4"/10cm) in St st.

Adjust needle size as necessary to obtain correct gauge.

Special Techniques

Bind-Off in I-cord: Using needles two to three sizes larger than main needles, CO 3 extra sts at beg of BO row, *k next 2 sts and sl the 3rd st knitwise, then k 1 more st (4 sts on right needle). Pass the slipped st over the last knitted st (3 sts on right needle). Sl these 3 sts back onto left needle purlwise. Tug on working yarn to tighten up sts. Rep from * until only 3 sts remain. Cut yarn and draw through remaining sts.

Special Abbreviations

A = Head circumference (20"/51cm or desired size)

B = Earlobe (10"/25.5cm height over head to earlobe or desired height)

Project Notes

To customize hat, make strip of squares shorter than you desire, as Garter stitch is stretchy.

If hat is "deep" and will measure more than measurement B, then customize hat by skipping or working fewer hem edge Garter stitch ridges.

For flat top of hat, skip the plain knit row between decrease rows.

Block hat on a balloon blown to measurement A.

Use needles two to three sizes larger than main needles in your right hand to do I-cord BO.

If using multiple yarns, remember to change colors whenever you like. Try using different textures as well as colors

Instructions
Domino Section

First Strip

Square 1: CO 20 sts.

Row 1 and all odd rows (WS): K to last st, sl 1 wyif.

Row 2 (RS): K8, K2tog, ssk, k8.

Row 4: K7, k2tog, ssk, k7.

Row 6: K6, k2tog, ssk, k6.

Row 8: K5, k2tog, ssk, k5.

Row 10: K4, k2tog, ssk, k4.

Row 12: K3, k2tog, ssk, k3.

Row 14: K2, k2tog, ssk, k2.

Row 16: K1, k2tog, ssk, k1.

Row 18: K2tog, ssk.

Row 20: K2tog.

Note: Only cut yarn if you are changing yarn; no need to cut if using a self-striping yarn.

Square 2: Pick up and k10 sts along side edge; CO 10 sts—20 sts.

Work Rows 1–20 of Square 1.

Rep Square 2 until strip measure 1–2"/2.5–5cm less than measurement A, depending on desired fit. **Note**: This would be between seven and nine squares (sample is nine squares).

Second Strip

Square 1: CO 10 sts; pick up and k10 sts along side of Square 1 of First Strip—20 sts.

Work Rows 1–20 of Square 1.

Square 2: Pick up and k10 sts along Square 1 of Second Strip and 10 sts along edge of First Strip—20 sts.

Work Rows 1–20 of Square 1.

Rep Square 2 of Second Strip to match length of First Strip.

Sew strips together. Weave in ends.

Hat Top

With circular needle, pick up and k10 sts for every square made.

Example: Ten squares would equal 100 sts picked up (making sure the number picked up is a multiple of five).

Work 3 Garter st ridges. **Note**: Garter st in the rnd is k 1 rnd, p 1 rnd.

K 1 rnd; at the same time, starting at the beginning of the rnd, place 5 markers evenly around.

Rnd 1: *K to 2 sts before marker; k2tog; rep from * around.

Rnd 2: K 1 rnd.

Rep Rnds 1 and 2 until 5 sts remain, removing markers on last row and changing to dpns as needed.

Break yarn, leaving a 2-yard tail, and work tail through rem sts.

Top Knot

Using dpns and tail used for Hat Top, pick up and k4 sts.

Work I-cord for 2–2.5"/5–6.5cm. BO.

Weave in ends. Tie knot like a balloon.

Hat Hem

Pick up and knit the same number of sts as you did for Hat Top.

Work 3 Garter st ridges. BO in I-cord.

Weave in ends.

STAINED GLASS HAT DIAGRAM

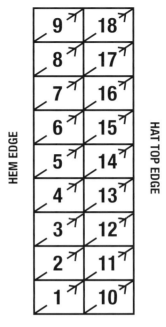

SEW EDGE TO EDGE OF 9 & 18

Note: Arrows indicate the direction of the decreases for each section.

DALA HORSE SWEATER

Anyone who has ever visited Sweden or the Swedish-settled communities in North America recognizes that the Dala horse is the unofficial but widely popular symbol of Sweden. The dear old horses have been carved as toys and gifts for children and grandchildren for centuries throughout Scandinavia and in other parts of the world.

Minnesota weaver Kelly Marshall created this bright and cheery geometric Dala horse weaving with its three-dimensional tail and mane using the traditional Rep weave technique, where the warp colors show the design and the weft is the binder that doesn't show. In the sweater, the basic horse pattern is worked in seed stitch and then afterwards a thread is worked in the purl bumps, similar to weaving, to create the stripes on the horse. Chain stitch is then worked around the horse outline and the tail and mane are tied on to complete the horse.

SIZES
Child's 2 (4, 6) years

FINISHED MEASUREMENTS
Chest: 22 (24, 26)"/56 (61, 66)cm

Length: 13 (14½, 15½)"/33 (37, 39.5)cm

MATERIALS 4
Cascade Yarns *220 Superwash Sport* (100% superwash merino wool, 50g/1.75oz, 136yds/124m): 3 (3, 4) skeins Red #809 (MC); 1 skein each Yellow #820 (A), Mint #1942 (B), Teal #845 (C)

Sizes 2 (2.75mm) and 4 (3.5mm), 16"/40.5cm long circular needles or size needed to obtain gauge

Size 2 (2.75mm) and 4 (3.5mm) double-pointed needles

Small size crochet hook

Stitch markers

Stitch holders

Piece of cardboard the same size as sweater

Tapestry needle

GAUGE
24 sts and 32 rnds = 4"/10cm in St st using larger needles.

Adjust needle size as necessary to obtain correct gauge.

Special Techniques

Kitchener Stitch (see Special Techniques Used, page 185)

Special Abbreviations

S2KP2: Slip 2 sts tog knitwise, k1, pass the slipped sts over (this is centered double dec).

Pattern Notes

Instructions for the Matching Stuffed Horse are given at the end.

Instructions

With smaller circular needle and MC, CO 116 (124, 132) sts. Pm for beg of rnd and join, taking care not to twist sts.

Work around in k2, p2 rib for 1½ (2, 2)"/4 (5, 5)cm. Change to larger circular needle.

Next Rnd: Knit, inc 12 (16, 16) sts evenly spaced around—128 (140, 148) sts.

Knit 5 (5, 7) more rnds.

Horse Motif

Rnd 1: With MC k7 (10, 12) sts, pm, foll chart across 50 sts working horse motif in seed st, pm. With MC k rem sts.

Cont as est, working horse motif in seed st and rem sts in St st until piece measures 7½ (8 ½, 9)"/19 (21, 23) cm from CO.

Divide for Armholes

Place the last 64 (70, 74) sts on circular needle or holder for back.

Front

Cont working back and forth on the rem 64 (70, 74) sts for front until horse motif is complete. Then cont working back and forth on front sts in St st until piece measures 3 (3½, 4)"/7.5(9, 10)cm from armhole split. Place center 14 (18, 20) sts on holder for neck, leaving 25 (26, 27) sts on each side of neck on needle.

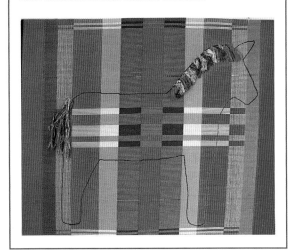

Left Neck Shaping

Row 1: K1, ssk, k to end.

Row 2: P.

Rep Rows 1 and 2 until 20 sts rem.

Cont even in St st until armhole measures 5½ (6, 6½)"/14 (15, 16.5)cm. Place rem sts on holder.

Right Neck Shaping

Row 1: K to within 3 sts from end, k2tog, k1.

Row 2: Purl.

Rep Rows 1 and 2 until 20 sts rem.

Cont even in St st until armhole measures 5½ (6, 6½)"/15 (15, 16.5)cm. Place rem sts on holder.

Back

Place 64 (70, 74) back sts from holder onto needle. Work back and forth in St st until armhole measures 5 (5½, 6)"/12.5 (14, 15)cm. Place center 20 (26, 30) sts on holder for neck, leaving 22 sts on each side of neck on needle.

Rep neck shaping for left and right side as for fronts until 20 sts rem. Leave sts on needle. Place front sts on spare needle and work Kitchener stitch or three-needle bind-off to join shoulders.

DALA HORSE SWEATER DIAGRAM

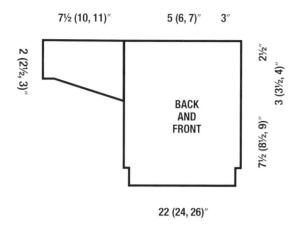

7½ (10, 11)"   5 (6, 7)"   3"

2 (2½, 3)"

2½"

3 (3½, 4)"

BACK
AND
FRONT

7½ (8½, 9)"

22 (24, 26)"

Sleeves

Note: The sleeves are worked in a seed st and stripe pat. The first rnd of the new color is knit; the next 7 rnds are worked in seed st as est.

With RS facing, using A and larger dpns, pick up and k60 (66, 72) sts around armhole.

Pm in first st (this will be the center underarm st) and join.

Rnd 1: *K1, p1; rep from * to end of rnd.

Rnd 2: Work in seed st, having a p st over a k st and a k st over a p st and ending 1 st before end of rnd.

Rnd 3: S2KP2, work rem sts in est seed st.

Rnds 4–6: Rep Rnds 1–3 once.

Rnd 7: Work in seed st.

Change to B.

Rnd 1: Knit.

Rnds 2–7: Rep Rnds 1–3 of A stripe twice.

Rnd 8: Work in seed st.

Change to C.

Rnd 1: Knit.

Rnds 2–7: Rep Rnds 1–3 of A stripe twice.

Rnd 8: Work in seed st.

Cont to work the stripe/seed pat, alternating colors A, B, and C every eight rows and at the same time, working the centered dec every 3rd rnd until 40 (48, 52) sts rem. Work in est stripe sequence until sleeve measures 6 (8, 9)"/15 (20.5, 23) cm from beg.

Change to MC, and smaller dpns.

Next Rnd: K, dec to 36 (44, 48) sts. Work around in k2, p2, ribbing for 1 ½ (2, 2)"/4 (5, 5)cm. BO in ribbing.

Finishing
Block sweater to desired dimensions.

Dala Horse "Weaving"
Cut a piece of cardboard to match the sweater size. Slide cardboard inside body of the sweater. Starting at the left side of horse and leaving a long tail for the chain st detail, use a blunt tapestry needle to weave the yarn under each purl bump along the length of the horse pat (shown in photo). Weave five columns of each color inside the horse pat. Work chain sts around the outside edges of horse.

Fringe Detail

Using one length of each pastel color, fold yarn over crochet hook and pull loop through chain sts; place ends through folded end and pull to secure. Place fringe along the back of neck for mane.

Tail

Cut twelve lengths, four of each pastel color. Fold yarns over crochet hook and pull loop through chain sts at tail of horse; place ends through folded end and pull to secure. If there is a concern about the tail being pulled off by child, it can be secured by sewing on the inside.

Matching Stuffed Horse

Follow the Dala Horse Garland pat (see page 88) but double the MC and use size 8 (5mm) double-pointed needles to make this larger horse. Omit the Lazy Daisy and Zigzag stitch embroidered on the horse. Sew mane and tail in similar fashion as on the sweater.

DALA HORSE SWEATER CHART

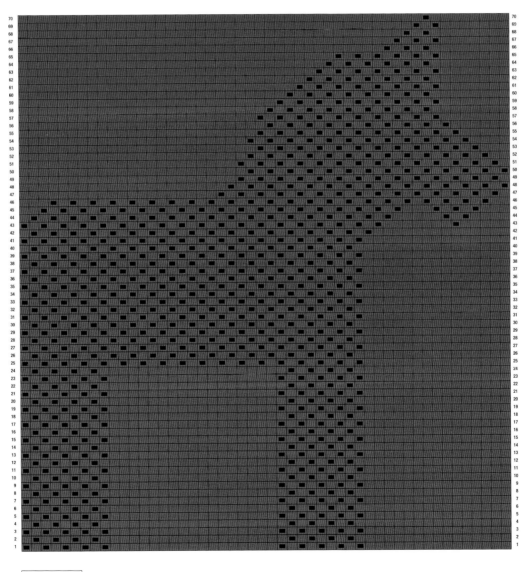

KEY
- MC Knit
- MC Purl

DALA HORSE GARLAND

The distinctive style of folk painting called *Dalmälning* originated in the province of Dalarna, Sweden. The Dalarna folk painting was first practiced in churches as a form of decorative storytelling. The painting style, which was originally used to teach Bible stories to parishioners, evolved into a means of commemorating important events like weddings.

The migration of the painting style to the carved horse is said to have started when a Dala painter, Stlkä Eric Hansson, was disabled. Since he was no longer able to paint walls, he sold the painted horses to help support his family. The carved horse with the "fancy flower painting" has been adopted as a symbol of Sweden.

FINISHED MEASUREMENTS
Horse Width: 2"/5cm

Horse Height: 3"/7.5cm

MATERIALS 4
Cascade Yarns *220 Superwash Sport* (100% superwash merino wool, 50g/1.75oz, 136yds/124m): 1 skein Red #809 (MC); small amounts of Yellow #820 (A), Mint #1942 (B), Teal #845 (C), #803 Navy (D)

Size 2 (2.75mm) double-pointed needles or size needed to obtain gauge

Small size crochet hook

Tapestry needle

GAUGE
24 sts and 32 rows = 4"/10cm in St st.

Adjust needle size as necessary to obtain correct gauge.

Special Techniques
Kitchener Stitch (see Special Techniques Used, page 185)

Instructions
First Leg
With MC, CO 12 sts. Pm at beg of rnd and join, taking care not to twist sts.

Rnds 1–12: Knit.

Rnd 13: BO 2 sts, k to end.

Place rem 10 sts on holder.

Second Leg
Work same as first leg, leaving sts on needles.

Belly
With MC, CO 7 sts for belly at end of last needle, place sts from first leg onto needles and knit them, CO 7 more sts for belly, and cont to k5 sts from second leg, joining to form a circle—34 sts. Pm here for center back and beg of rnd.

Note: The opening that was created by the CO sts and the leg BO is for stuffing the horse.

Body
Rnds 1–9: Knit.

Rnd 10: K1, ssk, k to within 3 sts from end, k2tog, k—32 sts.

Rnd 11: Knit. Fold in half at center back marker and, using Kitchener stitch, weave 14 sts tog (7 sts from each side) to form back of horse. Keep marker at center back.

Rnd 12: K9, at center front CO 10 sts, k to end—28 sts. **Note:** The hole that forms on the center back will be covered up with an embroidered flower later.

Rnd 13: Knit.

Rnd 14: K1, ssk, k10, k1f&b of next 2 sts, k10 , k2tog, k1—28 sts.

Rnd 15: K13, k1f&b of next 2 sts, k13—30 sts.

Rnd 16: K1, ssk, k24 , k2tog, k1—28 sts.

Rnd 17: Knit.

Rnd 18: K1, ssk, k9, k2tog, ssk, k9, k2tog, k1—24 sts.

Rnd 19: K10, k2tog, ssk, k10—22 sts.

Rnd 20: K1, ssk, k6, k2tog, ssk, k6, k2tog, k1—18 sts.

Rnd 21: K7, k2tog, ssk, k7—16 sts.

Rnd 22: K1, ssk, k3, k2tog, ssk, k3, k2tog, k1—12 sts.

Rnd 23: K4, k2tog, ssk, k4—10 sts.

Rnd 24: K1, ssk, k2tog, ssk, k2tog, k1—6 sts.

Rnds 25–26: Knit, thread rem sts onto yarn, and pull tight for ear.

Sew chin and leg openings closed, stuff with fiberfill, and sew belly.

Weave in all ends.

Garland Cord
With double strand of D and dpns, CO 4 sts, knit, *without turning work, slide sts to other end of needle, knit, rep from * for approximately 64"/162.5cm.

Finishing

With A, B, or C, work one Lazy Daisy stitch on the back of the horse. With an alternating color, make three or four French knots in the center of flower. With C or D, work zigzag stitch around horse for harness. Cut 12"/30.5cm strands of A and D. Thread one strand of A and D through center neck, braid, and use ends to attach horse to Garland Cord.

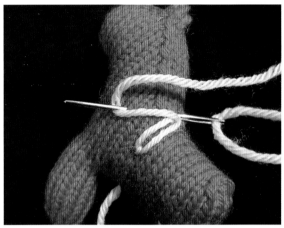

Lazy Daisy, step 1

Lazy Daisy, step 2

French knot

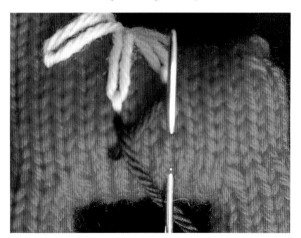

Zigzag stitch

MANLY MANSION MUFFLER

The stonework at the American Swedish Institute inspired this cozy scarf, which replicates the big and little repeat design in the mansion's limestone block pattern. The scarf is knit using the double-knitting technique, not to be confused with DK weight yarn! Although this muffler was designed for a man, it would be perfect for woman as well. Choose the Blackberry Ridge yarn we used (a slightly "toothy" natural-colored wool) or a slick, soft merino and this pattern will be a great layer for your winter wearing! Our thanks go out to Nancy Lindberg, from whom we learned this technique, and to Debbie Stoller, for making it hip again.

FINISHED MEASUREMENTS
Width: 7"/18cm

Length: 52"/132cm

MATERIALS 2
Blackberry Ridge *Natural Colored* (100% wool, 4oz/113g, 350yds/320m): 1 skein each Dark Grey (MC) and Brown (CC)

Size 8 (5mm), 36"/91.5cm long circular needles or size needed to obtain gauge (2)

Tapestry needle

GAUGE
14 sts and 20 rows = 4"/10cm.

Adjust needle size as necessary to obtain correct gauge.

Special Techniques

Crochet Cast-On (see Special Techniques Used, page 185)

Pattern Notes

Double knitting is working both sides in one row. The chart represents the side facing you. For each square there is a knit stitch for the side facing you of the color indicated on the chart and a purl stitch for the other side in the opposite color. Therefore each stitch is really two stitches—one front stitch in knit and one back stitch in purl.

At the beginning of each row you will need to twist the two colors to close each end.

Instructions

Using crochet cast-on method and MC, CO 362 sts (multiple of 60 + 2).

Set-Up Row: (K1 MC, p1 CC) across row.

Using stranded method of choice, beginning with Chart Row 1, sl first st; *with both colors in back, k the st in color indicated on chart; with both colors in front, p the back st in opposite color; rep from * across each st on chart to last st; with both colors in front, p last st with both colors.

Cont working in double knitting, rep Chart Rows 1–17 twice.

BO Row: *With MC, k1, p1 and pass first st over second st to BO; rep from * across row.

Finishing

Weave in ends.

Manly Mansion Muffler Chart

Note: In double knitting, charts show only the RS of the pattern, but remember that each box on the chart actually represents two stitches: the right side as shown and the "hidden" back side. Once you've knit the RS stitch in the color shown, remember to purl the WS stitch in the opposite color.

MANLY MANSION MUFFLER CHART

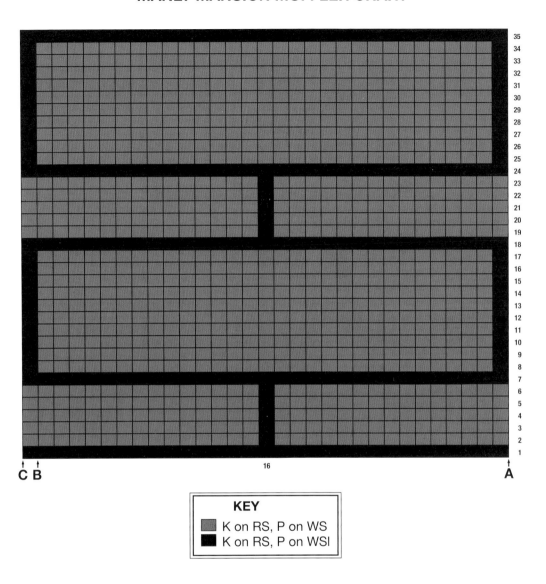

KEY

K on RS, P on WS

K on RS, P on WSI

PIPER'S HAT

In the 1930s, Evelyn Paulson embroidered a depiction of a Swedish bridal procession onto a long piece of linen fabric. The scene includes a wedding party with people in folk costumes. This wall hanging, a Works Progress Administration handcraft project, was part of FDR's New Deal to support the arts. This particular piece hung in the Bridgeview School in St. Paul, Minnesota, and was donated to the American Swedish Institute by Donna Flug in 1984.

The colors used in this wall hanging are indicative of the Depression era, a time when people used the materials that were available to them because resources were very limited. The New Deal version of the hat is knit with the traditional colors used in the original embroidered piece. The modern version of the hat is made using more contemporary colors. Both color combinations are fun to make and wear.

SIZE
Adult's average

FINISHED MEASUREMENTS
Circumference: 20"/51cm

Height: 12"/30.5cm (from top of hat to tip of earflap)

MATERIALS 🧶4🧶
Cascade Yarns *220* (100% wool, 100g/3.5oz, 220yds/201m)

New Deal version: 1 skein each Pink Heather #2451 (MC), Light Blue #7816 (A), Navy #7818 (B), White #8505 (C), Gold #8412 (D)

Modern version: 1 skein each Purple #7803 (MC), Teal #9421 (A), Navy #7818 (B), Light Blue #7816, Shrek #8903 (D)

Size 7 (4.5mm), 16"/40.5cm long circular needle or size needed to obtain gauge

Size 7 (4.5mm) double-pointed needles

Stitch markers (4)

Safety pins (2)

Tapestry needle

GAUGE
18 sts and 22 rnds = 4"/10cm in St st.

Adjust needle size as necessary to obtain correct gauge.

Special Abbreviations
S2KP2: Slip 2 sts tog knitwise, k1, pass the slipped sts over (this is a centered double dec).

Pattern Notes
The hat is constructed in one piece, including the earflaps. The earflaps are formed by a centered double decrease on each side of the hat. Note that the earflaps are set toward the back of the hat and not centered, to provide better coverage over the ears.

Instructions

With MC, CO 148 sts. Pm for beg of rnd and join, taking care not to twist sts.

Rnd 1: Knit.

Rnd 2: Purl.

Rnd 3: Attach A; knit, placing safety pin in the 31st and 118th sts to mark the center dec for each earflap.

Rnd 4: With A, purl.

Rnd 5: *With MC, k to 1 st before marked st; S2KP2; rep from * once, k to end—144 sts.

Rnd 6: *With B, k to 1 st before marked st; S2KP2; rep from * once, k to end—140 sts.

Rnd 7: *With B, p to 1 st before marked st; S2KP2;. rep from * once, p to end—136 sts.

Rnds 8–9: *With MC, k to 1 st before marked st; S2KP2; rep from * once, k to end—128 sts.

Rnd 10: *With C, k to 1 st before marked st; S2KP2; rep from * once, k to end—124 sts.

Rnd 11: *With C, p to 1 sts before marked st; 2SKP2; rep from * once, p to end—120 sts.

Rnds 12–14: *With MC, k to 1 st from marked st; S2KP2; rep from * once, k to end—108 sts.

Rnd 15: *With D, k to 1 st before marked st; S2KP2; rep from * once, k to end—104 sts.

Rnd 16: *With D, p to 1 sts before marked st; S2KP2; rep from * once, p to end—100 sts.

Rnds 17–19: *With MC, k to 1 st before marked st; S2KP2; rep from * once, k to end—88 sts.

Rnds 20–33: Foll Chart A on 88 sts.

Rnds 34–47: Foll Chart B; on the last rnd of chart; work S2KP2 between every other zigzag pat as indicated—66 sts.

Top Dec Rnds

Rnd 1: *With B, knit.

Rnd 2: With B, purl.

Rnds 3–5v With MC, knit.

Rnd 6: With D, *S2KP, k3; rep from * around—44 sts.

Rnd 7: With D, purl.

Rnds 8–10: With MC, knit.

Rnd 11: With C, *S2KP, k1; rep from * around—22 sts.

Rnds 12–14: With MC, knit.

Rnd 15: K2tog around—11 sts.

Break yarn, leaving a 6"/15cm tail. Using tapestry needle, thread tail through rem sts, pull tight, and secure ends.

Finishing

Weave in all ends. Block to finished measurements.

INSPIRED BY
Swedish Bridal Embroidery by Evelyn Paulson, American Swedish Institute Collection.

PIPER'S HAT CHARTS

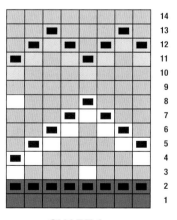

CHART A

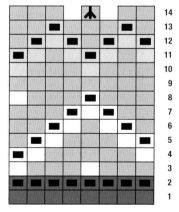

CHART B

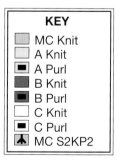

KEY

	MC Knit
	A Knit
	A Purl
	B Knit
	B Purl
	C Knit
	C Purl
	MC S2KP2

HILMA'S GLOVES

These gloves are named after Hilma Berglund, daughter of Swedish immigrants and co-founder of the Minnesota Weaver's Guild. The repeating pattern was inspired by Hilma's notebook, which contains many graphs and notes on weaving patterns. The weaving pattern has been knit vertically in three colors to create optical striping along the length of the glove. The saying "One life isn't enough for all the things I'd like to do" is a quote from Hilma's journal and is very appropriate for any fiber artist.

SIZE
Adult's medium

FINISHED MEASUREMENTS
Circumference: 7½"/19cm

Length: 11"/28cm (can be adjusted based on finger length)

MATERIALS
Brown Sheep *Nature Spun Fingering* (100% wool, 50g/1.75oz, 310yds/283m): 1 skein each Aran #N91 (MC), Scarlet #N48 (A), Evergreen #N24 (B), Off-white (MC), Red (A), Forest (B)

Size 1 (2.25mm) double-pointed needles (set of 5) or size needed to obtain gauge

Waste yarn or stitch holder

Stitch markers (one CC for beg of rnd)

Tapestry needle

GAUGE
48 sts and 44 rows = 4"/10cm in stranded 2-color St st.

Adjust needle size as necessary to obtain correct gauge.

Pattern Notes

The pattern is written for the right glove, which contains the quote. The left glove can be made with only the repeating pattern, the quote, or create your own special message.

Instructions

With MC, CO 88 sts, distributed evenly on 4 dpns. Pm for beg of rnd and join, taking care not to twist sts.

Main Glove

Rnds 1–53: Join A and foll Chart A, joining B as needed.

Thumb Opening

Right Glove—Rnd 54: With waste yarn k22 sts; slip these back to left needle, then cont Rnd 54 as charted.

Left Glove—Rnd 54: K22 sts, k22 sts with waste yarn, then cont Rnd 54 as charted.

Both Gloves—Center Hand Section

Rnds 55–82: Cont to foll Chart A.

Pointer Finger

Rnd 83: Foll Pointer Chart, work 11 sts; place next 66 sts onto a stitch holder; CO 10 sts in pat placing marker in middle of CO sts; then work rem 11 sts—32 sts.

Cont to foll Pointer Chart until 1½"/13mm from desired length.

Pointer Finger Tip Decreases

Dec Rnd: K1, ssk, k to 3 sts from marker, k2tog, k1.

Rep dec rnd until 8 sts rem.

Break off yarn, leaving a 6"/15cm tail.

With tapestry needle, thread rem sts and pull tight; secure end on WS.

Middle Finger

Place 22 sts from front and 11 sts from back onto needles; pick up and k10 sts in pat along CO edge from Pointer Finger, placing SOR marker in middle of 10 pick-up sts; k11 sts in pat, CO 6 sts in pat, placing marker in middle of CO sts; k11 sts in pat.

Foll Middle Finger Chart until ½"/12mm from desired length.

Middle Finger Tip Decreases

Dec Rnd: K1, ssk, k to 3 sts from marker, k2tog, k1.

Rep dec rnd until 8 sts rem and finish as for Pointer Finger Tip.

Ring Finger

Place 22 sts from front and 11 sts from back onto needles; pick-up and k6 sts in pat along CO edge from Middle Finger placing SOR marker in middle of pick-up sts; k11 sts in pat; CO 4 sts in pat placing marker in middle of CO sts; k11 sts in pat.

Foll Middle Finger Chart until ½"/12mm from desired length.

Ring Finger Tip Decreases

Decrease Rnd: K1, ssk, k to 3 sts from marker, k2tog, k1.

Rep dec rnd until 8 sts rem and finish as for Pointer Finger Tip.

Pinky Finger

Place rem 22 sts on needles; pick up and k4 sts in pat along CO edge from Ring Finger, placing SOR marker in middle of pick-up sts.

Foll Pinky Chart until ½"/12mm from desired length.

Pinky Finger Tip Decreases

Decrease Rnd: K1, ssk, k to 3 sts from marker, k2tog, k1.

Rep dec rnd until 8 sts rem and finish as for Pointer Finger Tip.

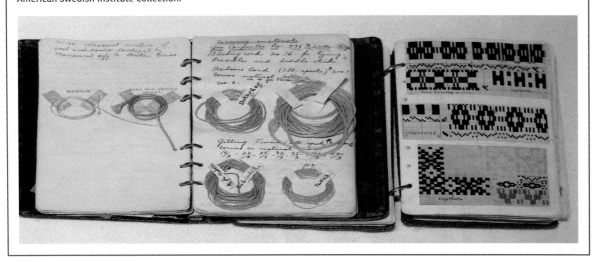

Thumb

Remove waste yarn and place live upper sts and lower sts on needles—44 sts.

Attach yarns and follow Thumb Chart until 1"/2.5cm from desired length. Pm after 22nd st.

Dec Rnd: K1, ssk, k to 3 sts from marker, k2tog, k1.

Rep dec rnd until 8 sts rem and finish as for Pointer Finger Tip.

Finishing

Weave in all ends. Block to finished measurements.

HILMA'S GLOVES CHARTS

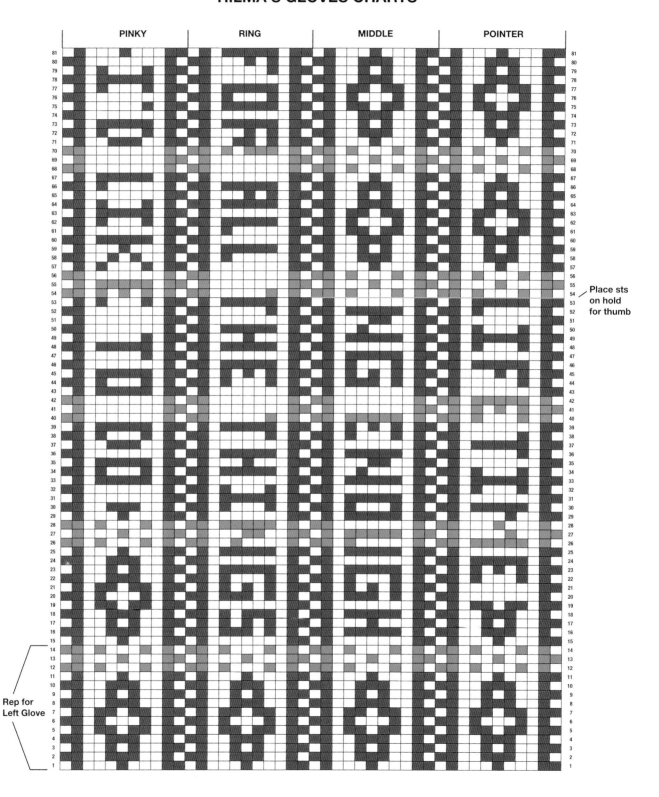

PINKY   RING   MIDDLE   POINTER

Place sts on hold for thumb

Rep for Left Glove

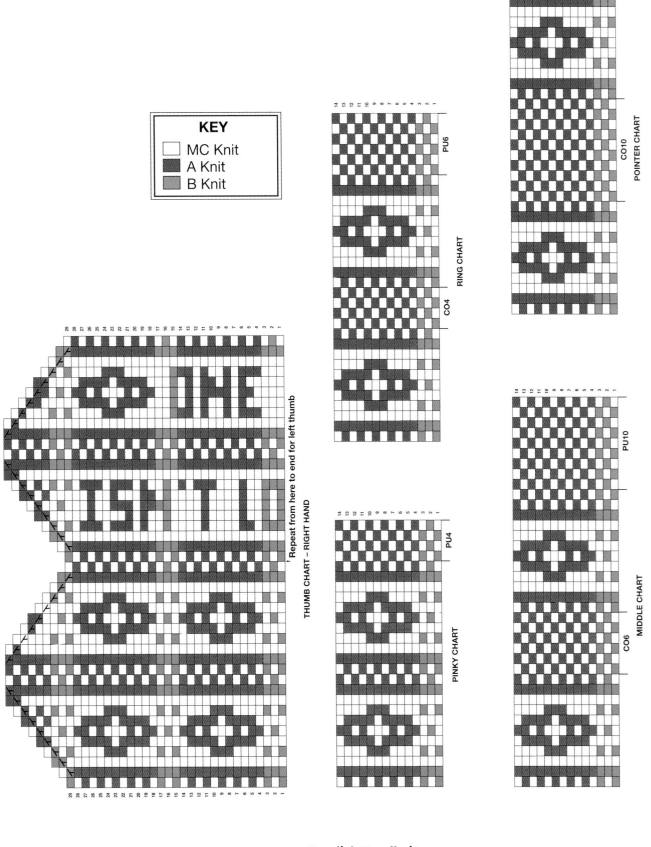

KEY
MC Knit
A Knit
B Knit

THUMB CHART – RIGHT HAND

Repeat from here to end for left thumb

RING CHART

PU6

CO4

PINKY CHART

PU4

MIDDLE CHART

PU10

CO6

POINTER CHART

CO10

HOPE CHEST SWEATER

This sweater crosses the border between Norway and Sweden. It is a marriage of Swedish-influenced weaving motifs and Norwegian knitting styles and techniques. We wanted to include items inspired by weaving in this collection, so when we found this piece of woven yardage, we knew we were on to something. The original yardage was woven by Silma Birch in 1905 for her hope chest. We assume it was in preparation for coming to America. The fabric is linen, spun from flax raised on her family farm. The original fabric is so beautiful, it's no wonder Silma never cut into it! We modeled the color pattern for this sweater after Silma's woven yardage. The solid section is created using a knitting motif that looks like weaving.

SIZE
Sweater is meant to be worn as a jacket and has one size. To make garment smaller or larger, adjust your gauge in Stockinette stitch and follow pattern.

FINISHED MEASUREMENTS
Bust: 54"/137cm

Length: 26"/66cm

MATERIALS 🧶4
Classic Elite Yarns *Liberty Wool* (100% washable wool, 50g/1.75oz, 122yds/112m): 16 skeins Deep Teal #7846 (MC); 4 skeins Gold #7850 (CC)

Size 8 (5mm) 32"/81.5cm long circular needle or size needed to obtain gauge

Size 7 (4.5mm) 32"/81.5cm long circular needle (or 1 size smaller than size needed to obtain gauge)

Size 7 (4.5mm) double-pointed needles (or 1 size smaller than size needed to obtain gauge)

Stitch markers (2)

Coilless pin-style stitch marker (1)

Buttons (9)

Tapestry needle

GAUGE
20 sts and 24 rows = 4"/10cm in St st on larger needles.

Adjust needle size as necessary to obtain correct gauge.

Special Techniques
Cable Cast-On

Three-Needle Bind-Off (see Special Techniques Used, page 184)

Two-Stitch One-Row Buttonhole: *Sl 1 purlwise, pass first slipped st over second st; rep from * once. Place last st back on left needle, turn. Using cable cast-on method, CO 3 sts, turn, sl next st to right needle, and pass the extra CO st over the slipped st.

Pattern Stitches
Mock Cable Ribbing (multiple of 4 + 2—see chart)

Basketweave Pattern (multiple of 18 + 10—see chart)

Transition Checkerboard Pattern (multiple of 4 + 2—see chart)

Large-Weave Stranded Pattern (multiple of 18 + 7—see chart)

Instructions
With MC and smaller needle, CO 270 sts. Join, being careful not to twist sts.

Rnd 1 (RS): K2, pm, beg Row 1 of Mock Cable Ribbing Chart (multiple of 4 sts + 2), working to 4 sts before marker, pm, k2.

Note: The 4 sts between markers are your steek sts. Beg of rnd is between these sts.

Cont to k the 4 steek sts and foll Mock Cable Ribbing pat for 2¼"/5.5cm or 8 reps.

Basketweave Pattern (Multiple of 18 + 10)
Knit 1 rnd, inc 10 sts evenly around—280 sts.

Change to larger needle, rep Basketweave pat for four and a half times or for 10¼"/26cm, keeping steek sts as est.

Transition Checkerboard Pattern (Multiple of 4 + 2)
With CC, work 4 rnds in garter st, inc 1 st each end of the 1st rnd once after and once before steek sts—282 sts.

Work Transition Checkerboard Chart once, keeping steek sts as est.

With MC work 4 rnds in garter st, dec 1 st in the 1st rnd, after steek sts—281 sts.

Large-Weave Stranded Pattern
(Multiple of 18 + 7)
Work Large-Weave Stranded Chart Rows 1–32 once, then Rows 1–27 once, keeping steek sts as est.

Place all sts on a holder for body of sweater. Weave in ends.

Sleeve (make 2)
With MC, and dpns, CO 48 sts. Pm at beg of rnd and join, being careful not to twist sts.

Work Mock Cable Ribbing for 2¼"/5.5cm or 8 reps, ending with Row 2.

Inc Row: K 1 rnd inc 1 st—49 sts.

Place coilless pin-style st marker on the 1st st.

Note: All incs will be done after the marked st at the beg of the rnd and before the marked st at the end of the rnd.

Rep Basketweave pat seven and a half times, ending on Row 9; at the same time inc every 3rd rnd, ending with a total of 139 sts.

Sleeve Facing
Work last rnd of sleeve to the last 2 sts, k2tog (these last 2 sts should include the center st). Beg working back and forth in Rev St st with MC. To personalize your sweater, chart the recipient's name in the sleeve facing using the instructions in the Alphabet Sleeve Facing instructions on page 105.

Row 1 (RS): Purl.

Row 2: K1, M1, k to last st, M1, k1.

Row 3: P1, M1, p to last st, M1, p1.

Rep Rows 2 and 3 twice more.

BO. Weave in ends.

Cut Neck
On front of sweater, mark off 40 sts on each side of neck for shoulders. Mark neck depth of 3"/7.5cm. Using a piece of cotton waste yarn, baste the shape of neckline around front of sweater. With machine, sew along the marked neck twice and cut out crescent, leaving ¾"/2cm seam allowance.

Cut Cardigan Front and Armholes
Using a contrasting color of cotton yarn, baste one line from side marker to marked armhole depth position, going between 2 center side edge sts, and another line down front of sweater between the 4 steek sts. (See Marking, Sewing, and Cutting a Steek on page 184. After sewing in sleeves, loosely sew facing to WS of armhole, covering cut edge.

Neckband
With RS facing, using MC and smaller needle, pick up and k32 sts along right neck edge, k62 sts of back neck, pick up and k32 sts along left neck edge—126 sts. *Do not join.*

Work in Mock Cable Ribbing for 4 reps.

Turning Row And Facing

**Row 1 (RS): Purl.

Row 2 (WS): Purl.

Row 3: Knit.

Rep Rows 2 and 3 three more times.

Rep Row 1.

BO.**

Using MC, loosely sew facing to WS of neck, covering cut edge.

Join shoulders, using three-needle BO.

Left Front Button Band

With RS facing, using MC, smaller needle, and pick-up method "3 sts for every 4 rows" or "2 sts for every 3 sts," pick up and k114 sts along Left Front edge for button band. Work Mock Cable Ribbing for 4 reps.

Rep from ** to ** on Neckband once for turning row and facing.

Right Front Buttonhole Band

Using same pick-up method as for button band, pick up and k114 sts along Right Front edge for buttonhole band. Work Mock Cable Ribbing for 1 rep, ending with a WS row.

Buttonhole Row: Work 8 sts in pat, *work Two-st Buttonhole (see Special Techniques on page 103), work 10 sts in pat, rep from * for a total of nine buttonholes.

Note: The placement of buttonholes is divided equally by two and a half MC reps.

Work 2 reps of Mock Cable Ribbing for a total of 4 reps, ending with a WS row.

Rep from ** to ** on Neckband once for turning row and facing.

Finishing

Using MC, loosely sew facing to WS of fronts, covering cut edge. Sew on buttons.

Weave in all ends. Block facings and bands.

Step 1: Chart out message on graph paper.

Step 2: Determine the center of the message and mark off the desired number of sts needed to center the message in the facing sts.

Step 3: Work facing in reverse St st, making sure that the first row is plain (not two-color). After completing the first row, add charted message to the next five rows. Knit final row in background color and thread sts onto yarn holder for sewing inside sleeve.

ALPHABET SLEEVE FACING CHART

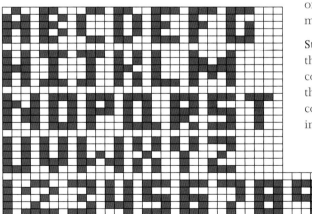

SWEDISH MITTENS TWO-COLOR KNITTING

We've been fascinated by the small, repeating motifs of Swedish mittens for quite some time. With a copy of Ingrid Gottfridsson's *The Mitten Book* in hand, we each set off to study the motifs, plotting which mittens to make first and dreaming of designing our own someday. So when it came time to design our version of Swedish mittens for this book, this particular motif quickly came to mind. The "XO" pattern is a symbol of fertility that is most often worn by women. Inspiration for this motif came from cross-stitches that were embroidered on the cuff of a blouse in the American Swedish Institute collection. This embellishment was thought to bring good luck to whomever wore the blouse.

The slanting cuff motif came from an old pattern by Joan Schrouder. Joan's pattern stated that a multiple of four for a 2x2 ribbing, plus one stitch, will make the ribbing slant to the left. Likewise, a 2x2 multiple ribbing, minus a stitch, will make the ribbing slant to the right. We added the extra color to add interest and make it unique.

SIZE
Adult's large

FINISHED MEASUREMENTS
Circumference: 8oz/20.5cm

Length: 10"/25.5cm

MATERIALS 1
Knit Picks *Palette* (100% Peruvian Highland wool,
    50g/1.75oz, 231yds/211m): 1 skein each Currant (MC)
    and Sweet Potato (CC)

Size 2 (2.75mm) double-pointed needles or size
    needed to obtain gauge

Stitch markers

Waste yarn (same size as mitten yarn or smaller)

Tapestry needle

GAUGE
32 sts and 33 rows = 4"/10 cm in St st.

*Adjust needle size as necessary to obtain the correct
    gauge.*

Instructions
Right Mitten

Cuff
With MC and dpns, CO 49 sts. Pm at beg of rnd. Divide sts evenly on dpns and join, taking care not to twist sts.

Knit 8 rnds.

Left-slanting ribbing: *With CC p2; with MC k2; rep from * for 24 rnds. **Note**: On all future rnds you will see that the ribbing jogs 1 st to the left.

With MC k 1 rnd, inc 11 sts evenly around—60 sts.

Purl 1 rnd.

Hand
Rnds 1–14: Work Chart A Rnds 1–14, reading chart from right to left.

Rnd 15: Work to red line for right thumb opening. Using waste yarn, k11 sts, transfer these 11 sts back to left needle, and cont to foll chart.

Cont to foll chart to tip of mitten, working dec rnds on chart as foll: K2tog, cont chart to last 2 sts, ssk.

Thumb
Carefully pull out waste yarn, placing sts on two dpns.

Note: You will have 11 sts on front needle and 11 sts on back needle. Foll Thumb Chart, working dec rnds on chart in same manner as for hand.

Left Mitten

Cuff
With MC and dpns, CO 47 sts. Pm at beg of rnd. Divide sts evenly on dpns and join, taking care not to twist sts.

Knit 8 rnds.

Right-slanting ribbing: *With CC p2; with MC k2; rep from * for 24 rnds. **Note:** On all future rnds you will see that the ribbing jogs 1 st to the right.

With MC, k 1 rnd, inc 13 sts evenly around—60 sts.

Purl 1 rnd.

INSPIRED BY

The cross-stitched motif on the edge of this folk costume is said to be a fertility symbol commonly worn by women. This motif inspired the stitch design used in the Swedish Mittens. American Swedish Institute Collection.

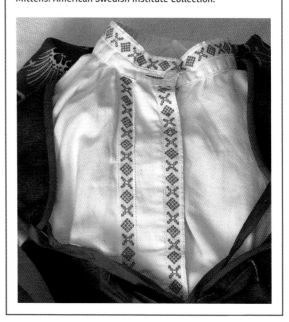

Hand
Rnds 1–14: Work Chart A Rnds 1–14, reading chart from right to left.

Rnd 15: Work to red line for left thumb opening. Using waste yarn, k11 sts; transfer these 11 sts back to left needle and cont to foll chart.

Cont to foll chart to tip of mitten working dec rnds on chart as foll: K2tog, cont chart to last 2 sts, ssk.

Thumb
Carefully pull out waste yarn, placing sts on 2 dpns. **Note:** You will have 11 sts on front needle and 11 sts on back needle. Foll Thumb Chart working dec rnds on chart in same manner as for hand.

Finishing
Weave in all ends. Block to finished measurements.

SWEDISH MITTENS CHARTS

CHART A

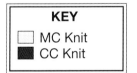

KEY
- ☐ MC Knit
- ■ CC Knit

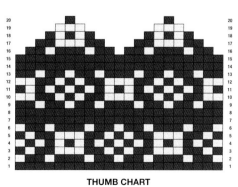

THUMB CHART

BOHUS-INSPIRED BIRCH TREE HAT

This birch tree hat offers a new twist on the Bohus tradition. Bohus knitting is often thought of as a rhythmic repeat of short patterns, using purl stitches to blend many similar hues and create a gradation of color. It is less known that in the early years of the Bohus cooperative, embroidery was also used on a number of the plain mitten designs to enhance the texture and add decoration. Both purl stitches and embroidery are used in this hat to achieve a unique reflection of the birch tree.

SIZE
Adult's average

FINISHED MEASUREMENTS
Head circumference: 20"/51cm

Length: 9"/23cm

MATERIALS 4
Cascade Yarns *220* (100% wool, 100g/3.5oz, 220yds/201m)

Rust version: 1 skein each Forest Green Heather #9486 (MC), White #8505 (A), Black #8555 (B), Rust #9460 (C), Green Heather #3176 (D)

Green version: 1 skein each Forest Green Heather #9486 (MC), White #8505 (A), Black #8555 (B), Lt. Green Heather #3176 (C), Green Heather #9460 (D)

Size 7 (4.5mm) double-pointed (set of 5) and 16"/40.5cm long circular needles or size needed to obtain gauge

Size 6 (4 mm) 16"/40.5cm long circular needle

Waste yarn

Stitch markers, two in CC (for beg of rnd and center stitch)

Tapestry needle

GAUGE
20 sts and 20 rnds = 4"/10cm in stranded two-color St st on larger needles.

Adjust needle size as necessary to obtain correct gauge.

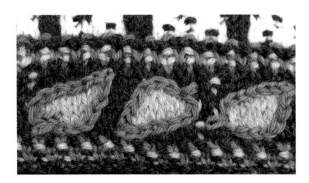

Special Techniques

Provisional Cast-On (see Special Techniques Used, page 185)

Kitchener Stitch (see Special Techniques Used, page 185)

Pattern Notes

Hat is worked in the round; change to dpns when stitches no longer fit comfortably on circular needle.

The facing is worked on a smaller needle to get a tighter fit; after brim pattern is complete, the facing is folded inside hat and fused to brim using a three-needle join technique.

INSPIRED BY

This oil painting, made by Axel Julius Gabriel Lindahl in 1932, inspired the Birch Hat. Lindahl was trained as a painter of theatrical backdrops, and the overall decorative quality of the painting gave us the idea to use the birch theme in a knitted item. American Swedish Institute Collection.

Instructions

Facing

With smaller needle and MC, and waste yarn, use crochet CO method, CO 112 sts. Pm for beg of rnd and join, taking care not to twist sts.

Knit 20 rnds.

Next Rnd (turning ridge): Purl.

Cuff

Change to larger needle.

Knit 1 rnd.

Attach C and work Chart A.

Attach D and work Chart B. Break off C and D.

Next Rnd (three-needle join): Remove CO sts from waste yarn and place them on smaller needle. Fold facing inside cuff so that WSs are tog. (The larger needle with cuff sts should be on the outside and the smaller needle with the facing sts should be lined up on the inside of the hat.) Holding needles parallel and using MC, *knit tog 1 st from the front needle and 1 from the back needle; rep from * around until all sts are joined.

Next Rnd: With MC, purl and dec 4 sts evenly spaced on the last rnd—108 sts. Pm after 54th st to mark center.

Main Hat

Rnds 1–30: Work 30 rnds foll Bohus Birch Chart C.

Rnd 31 (dec): Maintaining the charted pat throughout decreasing, *k1, ssk, k to within 2 sts from m, k2tog; rep from * around—104 sts.

Rnds 32–41 (dec): Cont to work charted pat, rep dec rnd every rnd.

Rnd 42: Knit.

Break yarn, leaving a 12"/30.5cm tail.

Fold rem sts in half and join using Kitchener stitch; secure end on WS.

Finishing

Embroidery: With C, chainstitch an outline around each leaf motif on the hat band. Backstitch once for leaf stem.

Weave in all ends. Block to finished measurements.

BOHUS-INSPIRED BIRCH TREE HAT CHARTS

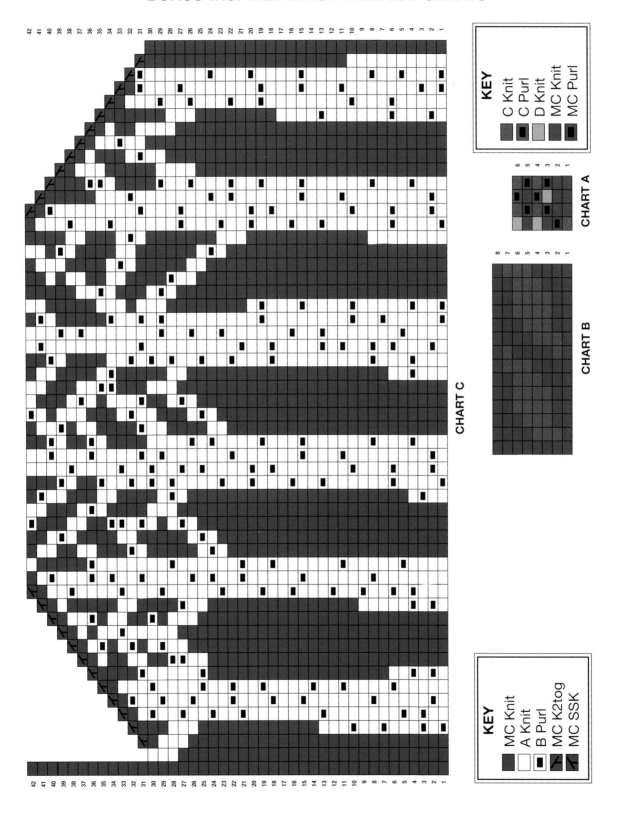

CHART C

CHART A

CHART B

KEY

	C Knit
■	C Purl
	D Knit
	MC Knit
■	MC Purl

KEY

	MC Knit
	A Knit
■	B Purl
◢	MC K2tog
◣	MC SSK

ALL THINGS SWEDISH SHAWL

We wanted to include in this collection a shawl, something that exemplifies all things Swedish, with unique motifs and a touch of whimsy. Twelve eyelet sections divide the shawl into "stories" of pattern. When the shawl is completed, a Scandinavian braid is woven through the eyelets and held in place with a button on each end.

FINISHED MEASUREMENTS
72"/183cm by 27"/69cm

MATERIALS 1
Karabella Yarns *Lace Merino* (100% merino wool, 50g/1.75oz, 255yds/229m): 9 skeins Color 642

Size 2 (2.75mm) 24"/61cm long circular needle or size needed to obtain gauge

Size 1 (2.25mm) 24"/61cm long circular needle (or 1 size smaller than size needed to obtain gauge)

Size C-2 (2.75mm) crochet hook

Scandinavian braid (9 yds/8m)

Buttons (24)

Cotton sewing thread for sewing buttons into place

Tapestry needle

Waste yarn

GAUGE
26 sts and 24 rows = 4"/10cm in St st.

Adjust needle size as necessary to obtain correct gauge.

Instructions

**Using waste yarn and provisional cast on, CO 137 sts.

Eyelet pat:

Rows 1–4: Knit.

Row 5 (RS): K2, *yo, k2tog; rep from * to last st, sl 1 wyif.

Note: If you are including the Scandinavian braid in your shawl, then the eyelet number *must* be an odd number.

Rows 6–7: K.

Row 8: K, *increasing* or *decreasing* as next pat indicates for next section.

Note: After all eyelet sections are complete you should be ready to work a RS row.

Santa Lucia Candles and Buns
To beg this section, you need 135 sts.

K4, work 9 sts of right-leaning Santa Lucia Bun motif, k4, work 5 reps of Candle Flame motif to equal 101 sts, k4, work 9 sts of left-leaning Santa Lucia Bun motif, k4.

Cont working charts as est, ending with a total of three Santa Lucia Buns on each side of 2 reps of Candle Flames.

Work 1 rep of Eyelet pat.

Woven Motif
On last row of Eyelet motif, dec 1 st across row—134 sts.

K 3 sts, work 8 reps of woven motif, k2, sl 1wyif.

Cont to foll chart for a total of 40 rows, ending with Row 8.

Work 1 rep of Eyelet pat.

Crowns
On last row of Eyelet motif, inc 1 st across row—135 sts.

Set-up Row 1 (RS): K3, MC2, k2, work crown motif over 121 sts (6 reps plus 1), k2, MC2, k2, sl 1wyif.

Set-up Row 2 (WS): K1, p2, MC2, p2, work crown motif over 121 sts (6 reps plus 1), p2, MC2, p2, sl 1wyif.

Work as est over 24-row rep twice and Rows 1–12 once.

Work 1 rep of Eyelet pat.

Hearts
To beg this section, you need 135 sts when starting Heart motif.

Set-up Row 1: K to last st, sl 1wyif.

Set-up Row 2: k1, p to last st, sl 1wyif.

Set-up Row 3: K3, *work Row 1 of Heart motif, k1; rep * across 5 motifs, k1, sl 1wyif.

Work Rows 1–17 of Heart motif once.

Ending Row: K1, p to last st, sl 1wyif.

Work 1 rep of Eyelet pat and on last row, inc 3 sts evenly across—138 sts.

Swedish Flags
To beg this section, you need 138 sts.

Set-up Row 1: K to Last st, sl 1wyif.

Set-up Row 2: K1, p to last st, sl 1wyif.

Set-up Rows 3 and 4: Rep set-up Rows 1 and 2.

Work Rows 1–12 of Flag motif fifteen times.**

Work 1 rep of Eyelet pat and on last row, dec 1 st—137 sts.

Sunspots, aka Meatballs
To beg this section, you need 137 sts.

Work Sunspots Chart four and a half times (Rows 1–24 four times and Rows 1–10 once).

Work 1 rep of eyelet pat and on last row of inc 1 st—138 sts.

P 1 row.

Place sts on a holder.

Return to beg of instructions and rep from ** to **.

K 1 row.

P 1 row.

Place other half of shawl on smaller needle. Holding needles with WS's tog, use Kitchener st to join the two halves tog.

Edging

Row 1: Sl 1, k1, (yo, k2tog) 2 times, (yo) 3 times, k2tog, yo, p2tog.

Row 2: Yo, p2tog, k1, Sl first st to right needle dropping the other two wraps, place back on left needle, (k1, p1) two times all in large loop, (k1, p1) two times, k1, p2tog.

Row 3: Sl 1, (k1, yo, k2tog) two times, k4, yo, p2tog.

Row 4: Yo, p2tog, k5, p1, k2, p1, k1, p2tog.

Row 5: Sl 1, k1, yo, k2tog, k2, yo, k2tog, k3, yo, p2tog.

Row 6: Yo, p2tog, k4, p1, k3, p1, k1, p2tog.

Row 7: Sl 1, k1, yo, k2tog, k3, yo, k2tog, k2, yo, p2tog.

Row 8: Yo, p2tog, k3, p1, k4, p1, k1, p2tog.

Row 9: Sl 1, k1, yo, k2tog, k4, yo, k2tog, k1, yo, p2tog.

Row 10: Yo, p2tog, k2, p1, k5, p1, k1, p2tog.

Row 11: Sl 1, k1, yo, k2tog, k5, yo, k2tog, yo, p2tog.

Row 12: BO 3 sts, sl the st from right needle back to left needle, yo, p2tog, k5, p1, k1, p2tog.

Corner of Edging

Place st marker 3 sts in from the corner of your picked-up edging sts and place marker 3 sts after the corner of your picked-up edging sts.

Work in edging pat to first marker.

*Work an even row as usual, except do not end with p2tog; instead, end with p1.

Work next odd row as usual.

Work next even row as usual.

Work next odd row as usual.*

Work from * to *, removing markers as you get to them.

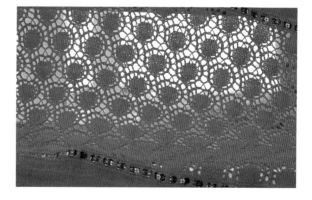

Cont edging pat to 3 sts before next corner, repeating directions for placing markers and turning corners a total of four times around shawl.

Finishing

Weave in all ends. Block to finished measurements.

Weave Scandinavian braid through eyelet pat, being careful not to pull braid too tightly. Use a button to hold braid down.

SWEDISH SHAWL CANDLES CHART

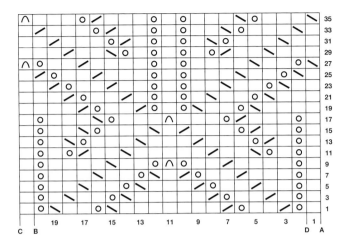

KEY

◣	SSK
◢	K2tog
○	Yarn over
⋀	SL1, K2tog, psso (-2)
☐	K on RS, P on WS

even rows 2-36: K1, P
across to last st, SL1wyif

SWEDISH LACE HEART CHART

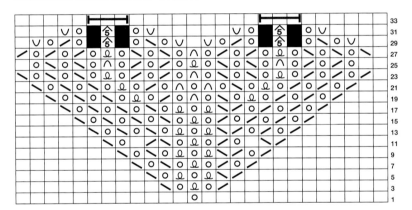

KEY

◣	SSK
◢	K2tog
○	Yarn over
℧	K tbl
■	No stitch
⋀	SL1, K2tog, psso (-2)
⋁	Inc 1
⑤	SSK, K3tog, pssk0
☐	K on RS, P on WS
⊢⊣	yf, s3 from L to R wise, yb, s3 wrapped sts back to L-ndl, K3

SWEDISH CROWNS CHART

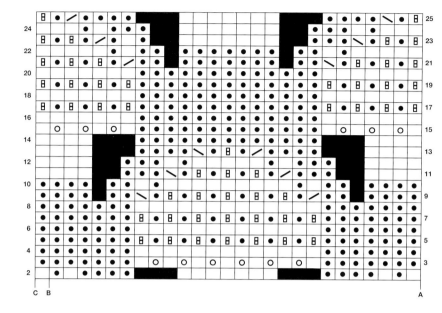

KEY

◣	SSK
◢	K2tog
○	Yarn over
•	P on RS, K on WS
■	No stitch
☐	K on RS, P on WS
🗄	Kltbl (K1 through back loop)
⌒	SL1, y0, K1, PSLS0

$_2$⌒^{3} Mock Cable (MC2) over 2 sts

20 + 1

SWEDISH FLAG CHART

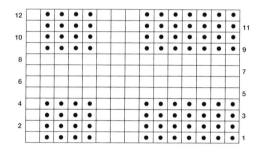

KEY

•	P on RS, K on WS
☐	K on RS, P on WS

Multiple 15

SWEDISH SUNSPOTS CHART

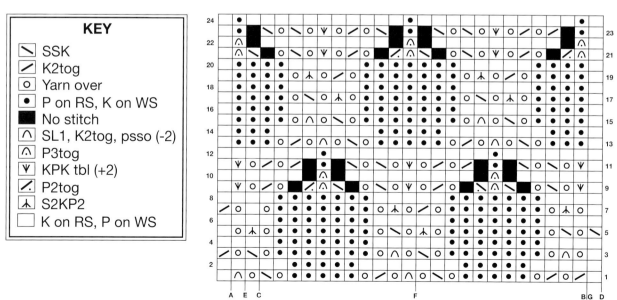

KEY

◣	SSK
◢	K2tog
○	Yarn over
•	P on RS, K on WS
■	No stitch
⋀	SL1, K2tog, psso (-2)
⌂	P3tog
ⱴ	KPK tbl (+2)
⧄	P2tog
⊼	S2KP2
☐	K on RS, P on WS

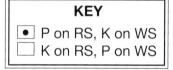

NORDIC KNITS

SHAWL WEAVE PATTERN CHART

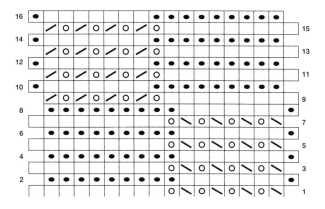

KEY

◣	SSK	●	P on RS, K on WS
◢	K2tog	☐	K on RS, P on WS
○	Yarn over		

SANTA LUCIA BUNS CHART

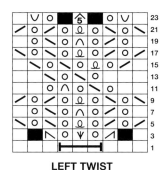

LEFT TWIST

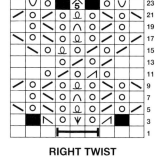

RIGHT TWIST

KEY

◣	SSK	⩒	KPK tbl +2
◢	K2tog	⋀	SL1, K2tog, psso (-2)
○	Yarn over	⋁	Inc 1
ℓ	K tbl	⑤	SSK, K3tog, pssko (-4)
⟋	K3tog	◤	K3tog tbl
■	No stitch	☐	K on RS, P on WS

⊢——⊣ yf, sl 3 sts from L to R need 6 p-wise, yb, sl 3 wrapped sts back to L needle, k3

even rows 2-24: K1, P across to last st, SL1wyif

TOMTEN WRISTERS

These wristers celebrate the folklore of the Swedish Tomte, mythical little men who take care of the farmstead. The name *Tomte* means "homestead man." The little man is child-sized and usually wears old clothes and a bright red hat. The Tomte take credit for clean and orderly farmsteads, although they will still cause mischief if denied their due of Christmas porridge.

SIZE
Adult's average

MATERIALS 🧶2
Cascade Yarns *220 Superwash Sport* (100% superwash merino wool, 50g/1.75oz, 136yds/124m): 1 skein each Blue #813 (MC), Ginger #858 (A), Black #815 (B), Red #809 (C), Taupe #873 (D), Cream #817 (E)

Sizes 3 (3.25mm) and 5 (3.75mm) double-pointed needles or size needed to obtain gauge

Size F-5 (3.75mm) crochet hook

Stitch marker

GAUGE
28 sts and 32 rnds = 4"/10cm in St st on larger needles.

Adjust needles as necessary to obtain correct gauge.

Instructions

With smaller dpns and MC, CO 60 sts. Pm for beg of rnd and join, taking care not to twist sts.

Rnd 1: Purl.

Rnd 2: *In one st k 5 sts wrapping yarn twice around needle (k1, yo, k1, yo, k1, yo, k1, yo, k1); rep from * around.

Rnd 3: *Slip each of the 5 double-wrapped sts onto the right needle dropping second wrap as they are slipped; return 5 long sts to left needle and p all 5 sts tog, p9, rep from * around—60 sts.

Rnd 4: *K1, ssk, k5, k2tog; rep from* around—48 sts.

Rnd 5: Purl.

Break off MC. Change to larger dpns.

Rnds 6–36: Work Chart A in St st, changing colors as indicated.

Break off A, B, C, D, and E. Change to small dpns.

Rnds 37–41: Attach MC, work around in k1, p1 rib.

Work crochet picot BO as foll: with crochet hook in right hand and needle in left hand, *using crochet hook, BO 4 sts, chain 3; rep from * around.

Break yarn and secure ends.

Finishing

Weave in all ends.

INSPIRED BY

The design for the bearded man is from a weaving made by Maj-Britt Westerberg. Westerberg's weaving is a traditional pattern from the Swedish area of Jämtland that features two styles of figures: one is the bearded man, and the other is a woman. The female figure could also be easily adapted for a second wrister, creating a his-and-her set of wristers. American Swedish Institute Collection.

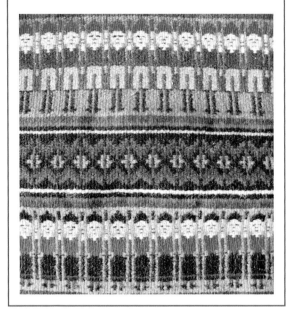

TOMTEN WRISTERS CHART

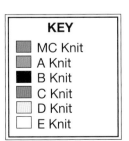

KEY

	MC Knit
	A Knit
	B Knit
	C Knit
	D Knit
	E Knit

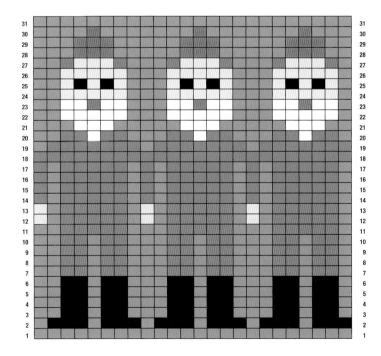

DAISY TOP

The inspiration for this design comes from the bodice of the Swedish National Costume: a blue twill vest with metal eyelets for lacing the bodice, which was decorated with white daisies and green stems. The vest and bodice were worn over a plain white shirt and a colored skirt with a daisy border.

This top is modeled after the vest but includes a row of daisies along the bottom as a reminder of the border on the skirt. It is knit in a beautiful linen-cotton blend that gives the piece an heirloom feel. The background stitch on the top is a modified linen stitch, which is reminiscent of hand-woven linen fabric.

SIZES
Women's small (medium, large, X-large)

FINISHED MEASUREMENTS
Bust: 32 (36, 40, 44)"/81.5 (91.5, 101.5, 112)cm

Length: 25 (26½, 27½, 29)"/63.5 (67.5, 70, 73.5)cm

MATERIALS 2
Louet *MerLin Sport* (60% linen/40% cotton, 100g/3.5oz, 250yds/228m): 1 skein each; Willow #55 (A), Cream #30 (B), Goldilocks #05 (C)

Size 4 (3.5mm) needles or size needed to obtain gauge

Waste yarn (to hold sts)

Stitch marker

Tapestry needle

GAUGE
28 sts and 36 rows = 4"/10 in pat st.

Adjust needle size as necessary to obtain correct gauge.

Special Techniques
Kitchener Stitch (see Special Techniques Used, page 185)

Pattern Stitches
Linen Stitch (worked in-the-rnd):

Rnd 1: *K1, yf, sl 1, yb; rep from * around.

Rnd 2: Knit.

Rnd 3: *Yf, sl 1, yb, k1; rep from * around.

Rnd 4: Knit.

Rep Rnds 1–4 for Linen St (worked-in-rnd).

Linen Stitch (worked back and forth):

Row 1: *K1, yf, sl 1, yb; rep from * across.

Row 2: Purl.

Row 3: *Yf, sl 1, yb, k1; rep from * across.

Row 4: Purl.

Rep Rows 1–4 for Linen St (worked back and forth).

Instructions

With MC, CO 240 (270, 300, 330) sts. Pm and join, taking care not to twist sts.

Border

Work Chart A (lace pat) for 7 rnds.

Next Rnd: *K13, k2tog; rep from * around—224 (252, 280, 308) sts.

Attach A and work Chart B (border pat) for 6 rnds. Break off A.

Attach B and work Chart C (daisy pat) for 14 rnds. Break off B.

Attach A and work Chart B (border pat) for 6 rnds. Break off A.

Body

Work Linen st in-the-rnd until piece measures 15 (16, 17, 18)"/38 (40.5, 43, 45.5)cm from CO edge, ending after an odd rnd.

Divide for Bodice

Using waste yarn to hold sts (or stitch holders), divide work as folls:

6 (6, 9, 9) sts for armhole, 50 (57, 61, 68) sts for right front, 50 (57, 61, 68) sts for left front, 12 (12, 18, 18) sts for armhole, 100 (114, 122, 136) sts for back, 6 (6, 9, 9) sts for armhole—224 (252, 280, 308) sts.

Note: The remainder of the top will be worked back and forth (flat) in Linen st.

Back Armhole Shaping

Turn work so that inside (WS) is facing and purl 100 (114, 122, 136) back sts.

Reestablish the Linen st pat working back and forth in rows; at the same time, work Dec Row every other row for 12 rows, then every 4th row for 24 rows as foll:

Dec Row (RS): K1, ssk, work Linen st as est until 3 sts from end, k2tog, k1.

Cont on rem 76 (90, 98, 112) sts until 7 (7½, 7½, 8)"/18 (19, 19, 20.5)cm from beg of armhole, ending with a WS row.

Back Neck Shaping

With RS facing, leaving first 30 (35, 37, 42) sts on needle for right back, place next 16 (20, 24, 28) sts on a holder for center back neck, then place last 30 (35, 37, 42) sts on a holder for left back.

Right Back Neck Shaping

Row 1: Work Linen st to within 3 sts from end, k2tog, k1.

Row 2: P1, p2tog-tbl, work Linen st to end.

Rows 3–12: Rep Rows 1 and 2, five more times—18 (23, 25, 30) sts.

Rows 13–14: Cont even in Linen st for 2 rows.

Row 15: Work Linen st to within 2 sts from end, k2tog, k1.

Row 16: Cont even in Linen st.

Rows 17–26: Rep Rows 13–16 five more times—12 (17, 19, 24) sts.

Right Shoulder Short Rows

Row 1 (RS): Cont in Linen st.

Row 2: Work 8 (12, 12, 16) sts, sl 1, yf, sl st back, turn and work back.

Row 3: Work 4 (6, 6, 8) sts, sl 1, yf, sl st back, turn and work back.

Place sts on holder.

Left Back Neck Shaping

Place 30 (35, 37, 42) left back sts from holder onto needle.

Row 1 (RS): K1, k2tog-tbl, cont Linen st to end.

Row 2: Work Linen st to within 3 sts from end, p2tog, k1.

Rows 3–12: Rep Rows 1 and 2 five more times—18 (23, 25, 30) sts

Rows 13–14: Cont in Linen st.

Row 15: K1, k2tog-tbl, cont Linen st to end.

Row 16: Cont in Linen st.

Rows 17–16: Rep Rows 13–16 five more times—12 (17, 19, 24) sts.

Left Shoulder Short Rows

Row 1 (RS): Work 8 (12, 12, 16) sts, sl 1, yf, sl st back, turn and work back.

Row 2: Work 4 (6, 6, 8) sts, sl 1, yf, sl st back, turn and work back.

Place sts on holder.

Right Front Armhole Shaping

Place 50 (57, 61, 68) right front sts from holder onto needle, attach yarn at center front, and purl row on WS.

Dec Row: K1, k2tog-tbl, cont Linen st to end.

Next Row: Cont in Linen st.

Rep Dec Row every other row for ten more rows, then every fourth row for 24 rows—38 (45, 49, 56) sts.

Right Front Neck Shaping

Work Linen st over the next 30 (35, 37, 42) sts; place rem 8 (10, 12, 14 sts) on holder for neckline.

Row 1: P1, p2tog-tbl, cont Linen st to end.

Row 2: Work Linen st to within 3 sts from end, k2tog, k1.

Rows 3–12: Rep Rows 1 and 2 five more times—18 (23, 25, 30) sts.

Rows 13–14: Cont in Linen st.

Row 15: Work to within 3 sts from end, k2tog, k1.

Row 16: Cont in Linen st.

Rows 17–26: Rep Rows 13–16 five more times.

Cont on rem 12 (17, 19, 24) sts until armhole is same length as outside edge of back armhole opening.

Right Shoulder Short Rows

Row 1: Cont in Linen st.

Row 2: Work 8 (12, 12, 16) sts, sl 1, yf, sl st back, turn and work back.

Row 3: Work 4 (6, 6, 8) sts, sl 1, yf, sl st back, turn and work back.

Place sts on holder.

Using Kitchener stitch, join right front and right back shoulders.

Left Front Armhole Shaping

Work same as Right Front Armhole Shaping to neck shaping, rev shaping.

Left Front Neck Shaping

Work same as Right Front Neck, rev shaping.

Left Shoulder Short Rows

Row 1: Work 8 (12, 12, 16) sts, sl 1, yf, sl st back, turn and work back.

Row 2: Work 4 (6, 6, 8) sts, sl 1, yf, sl st back, turn and work back.

Place sts on holder.

Using Kitchener stitch, join left front and left back shoulders.

Armhole Edging

Place 6 (6, 9, 9) underarm sts from holder onto shorter circular needle, then with MC pick up and k90 (90, 91, 91) sts around armhole—96 (96, 100, 100) sts. Pm and join.

Rnd 1: Purl.

Rnds 2–3: *K2 with MC, k2 with A; rep from * around.

Rnd 4: Purl.

Rnds 5–7: Knit.

BO. Fold facing over along Rnd 4 purl ridge and sew to inside edge.

Neck Facing

Place 8 (10, 12, 14) neck sts from holder onto shorter circular needle, then with MC pick up and k37 sts around neck to back; work 16 (20, 24, 28) sts from holder for center back, cont to pick up and k37 sts around neckline, work front 8 (10, 12, 14) sts from other side of neck—106 (114, 122, 130) sts.

Rnd 1: Knit.

Rnd 2: *K2 with MC, k2 with A; rep from *, end k2 MC.

Rnd 3: *P2 with MC, p2 with A; rep from *, end p2 MC.

Rnds 4–5: Purl.

Rnd 6: Knit.

Rnd 7: Purl.

BO. Fold facing over along Rnd 4 purl ridge and sew to inside edge.

Neckline

With A, knit applied I-cord around the neck slit. For eyelet holes, work 3 rnds of unattached I-cord, skip 3 rnds, then work 3 rnds of attached I-cord and so on, evenly spacing the eyelet holes along the slit.

Embroidery

With C, make a cluster of French knots inside each daisy around bottom of top.

With B, use the Lazy Daisy stitch to make three daisies on each side of front. Use the close-up photo as a guide for the placement of the flowers. For each leaf of flower make one large petal (Lazy Daisy) and one smaller petal inside the larger one. With C, make a cluster of French knots inside each flower. With A, use satin stitch to make two or three leaves around each daisy, making the edge of the leaf jagged by using long and short stitches.

Lace

With C, make an I-cord approx 36"/91.5cm length and lace through eyelets on neck slit.

Finishing

Weave in all ends. Block.

DAISY TOP CHART

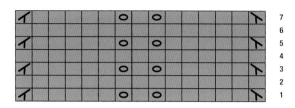

CHART A

CHART B

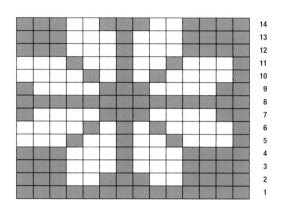

CHART C

KEY

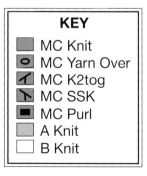

▨	MC Knit
◯	MC Yarn Over
⟋	MC K2tog
⟍	MC SSK
■	MC Purl
▨	A Knit
☐	B Knit

DAISY TOP

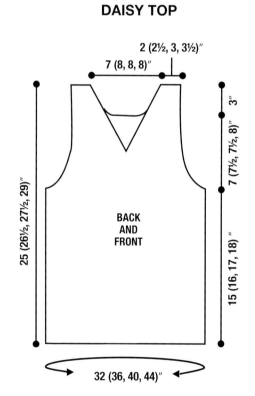

2 (2½, 3, 3½)"

7 (8, 8, 8)"

3"

7 (7½, 7½, 8)"

BACK AND FRONT

25 (26½, 27½, 29)"

15 (16, 17, 18)"

32 (36, 40, 44)"

CRAYFISH HOT PAD

The end of summer in Sweden is marked with an outdoor party featuring crayfish. The tradition of the crayfish feast or crayfish supper, held in the month of August, started in the mid-nineteenth century. In contrast to a Louisiana "crawdad" boil, Swedish crayfish are boiled with a mild dill flavor instead of the hot and spicy Cajun seasoning. The crayfish are boiled in a large pot over an open fire. It is perfectly acceptable, and in fact easier, to eat crayfish with your fingers, breaking off the tails, peeling, and eating. The crayfish feast is often accompanied with bread, cheese, beer, and schnapps.

The outdoor country setting of the crayfishing activities is depicted in the Carl Larsson painting of the same name. In *Crayfishing*, Carl's family is shown collecting crayfish with a net in one hand and bait suspended from a line in the other hand. The Larsson children appear to be doing all this while balancing on a small rock on the shoreline or while wading in the water.

FINISHED MEASUREMENTS
20"/51cm circumference by 12"/30.5cm height (from top to tip of earflap)

MATERIALS 4
Cascade Yarns *220* (100% wool, 100g/3.5oz, 220yds/201m): 1 skein #7818 Royal Blue (MC)

Cascade Yarns *220 Paints* (100% wool, 100g/3.5oz, 220yds/201m): 1 skein #9868 Flame (CC)

Size 7 (4.5mm) 16"/40.5cm long circular needle or size needed to obtain gauge

Crochet hook size G-6 (4mm)

Stitch markers (2)

GAUGE
20 sts and 28 rnds = 4"/10cm in St st.

Adjust needle size as necessary to obtain correct gauge.

Special Techniques

Continental Cast-On

Kitchener Stitch (see Special Techniques Used, page 185)

Fulling (see Special Techniques Used, page 185)

Pattern Notes

This hot pad is knit in the round as a tube and closed off at each end. It can also be knit in double knitting; the result will be a reversible positive-negative pattern.

Instructions

With MC, using continental cast-on with waste yarn, CO 106 sts. Pm at beg of rnd and after 53 sts, then join, taking care not to twist sts. Knit 1 rnd.

Follow Chart

Attach CC and work Chart Rnds 1–66 in St st.

Break off CC. With MC only, knit 1 rnd.

Finishing

Remove waste yarn from CO edge and place sts on needle. Using Kitchener stitch, close top of pot holder. Weave in all ends.

Full (felt) the piece by washing in warm water with mild soap, then agitate until it begins to look fuzzy. Dry flat.

CRAYFISH HOT PAD CHART

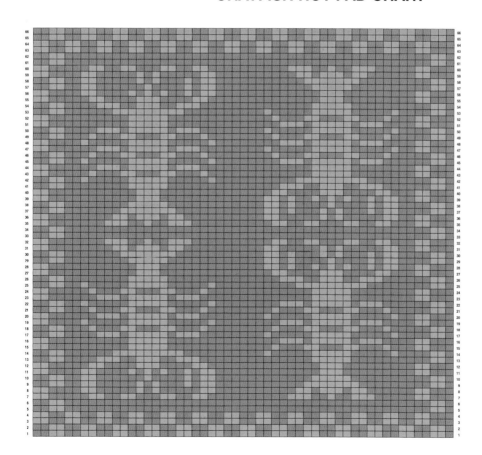

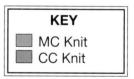

KEY
- MC Knit
- CC Knit

ICELANDIC
HANDKNITS

Icelandic tradition is full of beautiful handknits. All kinds of mittens with color-stranded work that have been decorated with cross-stitch: socks, caps, lace shawls, trousers, costumes, jackets with a great deal of shaping, underwear, inserts for shoes, blankets, pillows, and more. The abundance of so many different handknits is not at all surprising; there is indeed a rich tradition of knitting in Iceland, dating back to the early sixteenth century.

Evidence of this early knitting heritage can be found in district museums here and there throughout Iceland. Few pieces date back earlier than the nineteenth century, but the artifacts provide a good overview of traditional knitting in Iceland. The National Museum of Iceland in the capital city of Reykjavik has many knitted artifacts, but few of them are on display within the permanent collection, and you will have to wait for a special temporary exhibition to admire them. The Textile Museum in Blönduós, a town on the north shore of the country, however, displays one of the best permanent collections of handknits in Iceland.

Inspiration for the patterns on these pages came joyfully: Some are modernized designs, adapted to today's yarns and standards, while others are completely new and based on different artifacts discovered in various museum collections. All the designs have a recognizable traditional look but with a contemporary touch.

LEAF MITTENS, SLOUCHY CAP & SCARF

The motifs used in this hat, mitten, and scarf set are based on a type of mitten that is referred to as *vestfirdir* or *laufaviðar vettlingar*, meaning "mittens from the Westfjords" or "leaf mittens," respectively. I've always loved the colorwork in these mittens, and when I reinterpreted them with the Icelandic Kambgarn yarn (imported merino wool but Icelandic production), I was delighted by the result. The mittens fit very well with tip decreases starting at the little finger. The apparent lines of central double decreases are enhanced in the matching Leaf Slouchy Cap, where they make a pleasing structure at the top of the hat. The scarf is my new take on the classic garter stitch bow-tie scarf and is reminiscent of the bow tie worn with traditional Icelandic costumes.

NORDIC KNITS

MITTENS

SIZES
Women's small (medium) tight fit

FINISHED MEASUREMENTS
Hand circumference: 6¾ (7½)"/17 (19)cm

Hand length: 7½ (8)"/19 (20.5)cm

MATERIALS 🧶4
Ístex *Kambgarn* (100% new merino wool, 50g/1.75oz, 164yds/150m per ball): 6 balls #9652 brown (MC); 1 ball each #1204 light brown (CC1), #1213 dark blue (CC2), #1215 light blue (CC3), #1211 yellow (CC4), #9664 red (CC5), #0945 green (CC6), #0059 black (CC7)

Sizes 2 and 3 (2.5 and 3mm) circular needles

Magic loop is used for smaller diameters or double-pointed needles

Darning needle

GAUGE
28 sts and 36 rows = 4"/10cm in St st using larger needle

Adjust needle size as necessary to obtain correct gauge.

Special Abbreviation

S2sk = slip 2, slip 1, knit: Slip 2 sts as if to knit them together, slip 1 st as if to knit, insert left needle in the 3 sts and k3tog through the back loops (double central dec).

Note: Because of the double central decs, end of rnd moves 1 st to the left in those rnds, and you will have to replace your marker accordingly.

Mitten Instructions
Mittens (make two)

With CC7 and smaller needle, CO 44 (52) sts. Change to MC. Join, taking care not to twist sts in the rnd, pm EOR (end of rnd). Work around in *k1, p1* rib for 2"/5cm. Change to larger needle and work Pattern A1 (A2) from right to left (right mitten) or from left to right (left mitten), inc 4 sts in first rnd, [k11 (13), M1] 4 times—48 (56) sts.

Thumb Opening

Note: Mark thumb on Row 22 (24):

Right thumb: K1, k8 (9) sts with contrasting scrap yarn, place sts back on left needle and knit them again with MC, knit to EOR.

Left thumb: K39 (46), k8 (9) sts with contrasting scrap yarn, place sts back on left needle and knit them again with MC, knit rem st to EOR.

Tip: Work dec on both sides: *knit to 1 st before side st, s2sk* twice in every other rnd. End of rnd moves 1 st to the left in the rnds where the central double decs are worked.

When pattern is complete, 8 sts rem. Turn mitten inside out and BO using three needles on the inside, back to front.

Thumb

Remove scrap yarn and set sts on needle. With MC, pick up 2 extra sts (lifted inc) on each side of the hole and knit them together (double lifted dec, see Techniques) = 18 (20) sts. Following Chart B1 (B2), work even (= rep Rnd 1) in St st for about 1½ (2)"/4 (5)cm. Work dec on both sides in every other rnd:

Rnd 1: *Knit to 2 sts before extra side st, ssk, k1, k2tog* twice.

Rnd 2: Knit all sts.

Rep Rnds 1 and 2 until 6 (8) sts rem. Break off yarn and draw it through the sts.

Finishing

Weave in loose ends.

SLOUCHY CAP

SIZES
Adult's medium (large) to fit head
21 (24 ½)"/53.5 (62)cm

Finished Measurements
Head circumference: 20 (23)"/51
(58.5)cm

Note: You can achieve more sizes
by changing needle size.

MATERIALS
Ístex *Kambgarn* (100% new merino
wool, 50g/1.75oz, 164yds/150m
per ball): 6 balls #9652 brown
(MC); 1 ball each #1204 light
brown (CC1); #1213 dark blue
(CC2); #1215 light blue (CC3),
#1211 yellow (CC4), #9664 red
(CC5), #0945 green (CC6), #0059
black (CC7)

Sizes 2 and 3 (2.5 and 3mm)
circular needles

Magic loop is used for smaller
diameters or double-pointed
needles

Darning needle

GAUGE
28 sts and 36 rows = 4"/10cm in St
st using larger needle

*Adjust needle size as necessary to
obtain correct gauge.*

Special Abbreviation

S2sk = slip 2, slip 1, knit: Slip 2 sts as if to knit them together, slip 1 st as if to knit, insert left needle in the 3 sts and k3tog through the back loops (double dec).

Note: Because of the double central decs, end of rnd moves 1 st to the left in those rnds, and you will have to replace your marker accordingly.

Slouchy Cap Instructions

With CC7 and smaller needle, CO 144 (168) sts. Change to MC. Join, taking care not to twist sts, pm EOR (end of rnd). Work around in k1, p1 rib for 1"/2.5cm. Change to larger needle.

Rnds 1–69: Work Rnds 1–69 of Pattern A1, rep 6 (7) times across. When pattern is complete, 24 (28) sts rem.

Rnd 70: *S2sk, k1*; rep from * to * around—12 (14) sts.

Rnd 71: Knit all sts.

Rnd 72: *K2tog* around—6 (7) sts.

Break off yarn, draw it through the sts.

Weave in loose ends.

SCARF

SIZES
One size fits all

FINISHED MEASUREMENTS
Circumference: 16½"/42cm

Note: Size can be easily changed
by adding or removing rows.

MATERIALS
Ístex *Kambgarn* (100% new merino
wool, 50g/1.75oz, 164yds/150m
per ball): 6 balls #9652 brown
(MC); 1 ball each #1204 light
brown (CC1), #1213 dark blue
(CC2), #1215 light blue (CC3),
#1211 yellow (CC4), #9664 red
(CC5), #0945 green (CC6), #0059
black (CC7)

Sizes 2 and 3 (2.5 and 3mm)
circular needles

Magic loop is used for smaller
diameters or double-pointed
needles

Darning needle

GAUGE
28 sts and 36 rows = 4"/10 cm in St
st using larger needle

*Adjust needle size as necessary to
obtain correct gauge.*

Special Abbreviation

S2sk = slip 2, slip 1, knit: Slip 2 sts as if to knit them together, slip 1 st as if to knit, insert left needle in the 3 sts and k3tog through the back loops (double dec).

Note: Because of the double central decs, end of rnd moves 1 st to the left in those rnds and you will have to replace your marker accordingly.

Scarf Instructions

With MC and a provisional cast-on, CO 96 sts using larger needle. Work Pattern A1 (Rnds 1–69), rep 4 times across. When pattern is complete, 16 sts rem.

Next rnd: *K2tog* around—8 sts.

Break off yarn, draw it through the sts.

Remove provisional cast-on and with MC, *k2tog* across—48 sts. Divide sts in half and work separately: Knit first 24 sts back and forth in rib (k1, *p2, k2,* to last 3 sts, p2, k1) for 20 rows. Place on holder. Knit last 24 sts back and forth in rib (k1, *p2, k2* to last 3 sts, p2, k1) for 20 rows.

Cont knitting the 48 sts in the rnd:

Next rnd: *K1, M1* across—96 sts.

Work Stripes

Rnds 1–20: Work 20 rnds with MC same as Rnd 43 of Pattern A1.

Rnds 21–23: Work 3 rnds in colorway same as Rnds 18–20 of Pattern A1.

Rep these 23 rnds 5 times but with different colorway strip: alternatively like Rnds 24–26, 44–46, then again Rnds 24–26 and 18–20 of Pattern A1.

Work 20 more rnds with MC same as Rnd 43 of Pattern A1.

Note: You can work more or less than 20 rnds to achieve different length.

Work Pattern A1 (Rnds 1–69), rep 4 times across and work shaping like the other tip.

Finishing

Weave in loose ends.

Hand wash delicately in lukewarm water with gentle wool soap. Leave flat to dry.

LEAF CHART A1

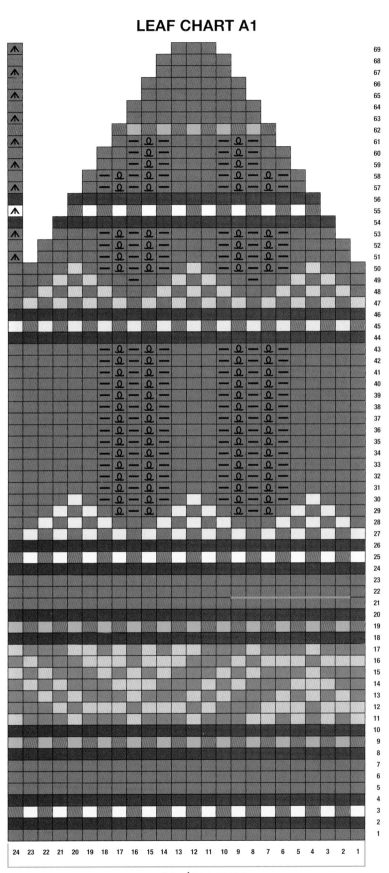

repeat twice across

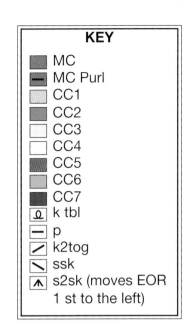

KEY

	MC
—	MC Purl
	CC1
	CC2
	CC3
	CC4
	CC5
	CC6
	CC7
Ω	k tbl
—	p
╱	k2tog
╲	ssk
⋀	s2sk (moves EOR 1 st to the left)

Thumb B1

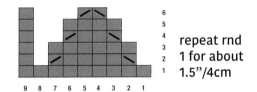

repeat rnd 1 for about 1.5"/4cm

mark thumb

LEAF CHART A2

mark thumb

rep rnd 1 for about 2"/5cm

Thumb B2

NORDIC KNITS

SKAGAFJÖRÐUR MITTENS

The mittens are inspired by a pair of mittens in the Textile Museum. They are decorated with an Old Icelandic cross-stitch flowerpot motif, typical from the fjord of Skagafjörður. I had to simplify and reduce the motif considerably to fit my mittens since they are knit with a much thicker yarn. My motif would probably fit on the thumb of the original pair! I did keep the same construction, however; they are knitted from the cuff up with a gusset and a star top. There is no left or right mitten, so keep this in mind when deciding on the placement of the embroidery.

SIZES
Women's small (medium)

FINISHED MEASUREMENTS
Hand circumference: 7¾ (8¾)"/19.5 (22)cm

Length of hand (without the cuff): 7 (8)"/18 (20.5)cm

MATERIALS
4 Ístex *Léttlopi* (100% pure Icelandic wool, 50g/1.75oz, 109yds/100m per skein): 2 skeins #0059 for black or #0051 for white (MC)

0 Ístex *Einband-Loðband* (70% Icelandic wool, 30% wool, 50g/1.75oz, 246 yds/225m per skein): scrap lengths in the color of your choice (CC) or see chart for suggestions

Size 4 (3.5mm) circular needle or double-pointed needles

Stitch markers

Tapestry needle

GAUGE
22 sts and 29 rows = 4"/10cm in St st using size 4 (3.5mm) needle

Adjust needle size as necessary to obtain correct gauge.

Pattern Stitch
Broken rib (multiple of 2)

Rnd 1: *K1, p1*.

Rnd 2: Knit all sts.

Rep Rnds 1 and 2.

Instructions
Mittens (make two)
With MC and size 4 circular needle, CO 32 (34) sts. Join, taking care not to twist sts; pm EOR (end of rnd). Work in around broken rib for about 2½"/6.5cm:

Rnd 1: *k1, p1* around

Rnd 2: K all sts.

Rep rnds 1 and 2.

Cont in St st: K2, pm, knit to EOR, then work inc for thumb gusset on both sides of markers as follows: *M1 on left side of EOR marker, knit to next marker, M1 on right side of it, knit to EOR, knit next 4 rnds* 4 (5) times—40 (44) sts.

Thumb Opening
Next rnd: K1, then k8 (10) sts with contrasting scrap yarn, place sts back on left needle and knit them again with MC, knit to EOR.

Cont knitting until mitten measures 4 (4½)"/10 (11.5)cm from thumb or 1"/2.5cm short of fingertips, then start dec:

Rnd 1: *K8 (9), k2tog* 4 times—36 (40) sts.

Rnd 2: *K7 (8), k2tog* 4 times—32 (36) sts.

Rnd 3: *K6 (7), k2tog* 4 times—28 (32) sts.

Rnd 4: *K5 (6), k2tog* 4 times—24 (28) sts.

Rnd 5: *K4 (5), k2tog* 4 times—20 (24) sts.

Rnd 6: *K3 (4), k2tog* 4 times—16 (20) sts.

Rnd 7: *K2 (3), k2tog* 4 times—12 (16) sts.

Rnd 8: *K1 (2), k2tog* 4 times—8 (12) sts.

Rnd 9 (Size S only): *K2tog* 4 times—4 sts.

Rnd 9 (Size M only): *K1, k2tog* 4 times—8 sts.

Rnd 10 (Size M only): *K2tog* 4 times—4 sts.

Break yarn and draw it through the sts.

Thumb
Remove scrap yarn and place the sts on the needle. Pick up an extra st on each of the outer corners of the thumb opening and k2tog with next st in next rnd—16 (20) sts. Work in St st for 18 (20) rnds, then start dec:

Rnd 1: *K2, k2tog* around—12 (15) sts.

Rnd 2 and every even rnd: Knit all sts.

Rnd 3: *K1, k2tog* around—8 (10) sts.

Rnd 5: *K2tog* around—4 (5) sts.

Break yarn and draw it through the sts.

INSPIRED BY
A collection of mittens, embroidered with a flowerpot motif in Old Icelandic cross-stitch, is typical of the embroidery from the fjord Skagafjörður. The Textile Museum in Blönduós.

Finishing

Weave in loose ends. Close the gaps at the outer corners of the thumb if needed. With CC, embroider the pattern in the middle of the back of the hand (when doing so, make sure to have a right-hand mitten and a left-hand mitten). Position the top of the embroidery at the 10th row from the top of the mitten and work your way down the center line of the motif, then out from center.

SKAGAFJÖRÐUR MITTENS CHART A1

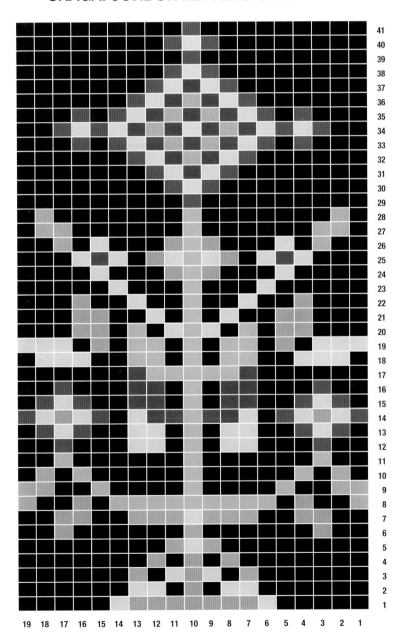

KEY

	embroider with Darker green 9112
	embroider with Light green 9268
	embroider with Gull/brunt 9075
	embroider with Orange 1766
	embroider with Dark red 9171
	embroider with Red 1770
	embroider with Blue 9281
	embroider with Pink 9128

NORDIC KNITS

SKAGAFJÖRÐUR TOTE BAG

The tote bag is inspired by the same pair of mittens I used to design the Skagafjörður mittens except the motif on the bag is an exact reproduction of the embroidery on the original mittens. The bag is spacious enough for a laptop with an inside pocket, a key chain, and a magnetic closure. It is knitted in the round in one piece and sewing is kept to a minimum. The bottom is knit as a tube with a sheet of plastic placed inside to make it sturdier. Stiches are picked up around the bottom. Handles are marked in the same manner as mitten thumbs, knitted in the round, and then grafted together.

FINISHED MEASUREMENTS
9½ by 1½ by 14"/24 by 4 by 35cm

MATERIALS
〔5〕 Ístex *Álafosslopi* (100% pure Icelandic wool, 3.5oz/100g, 109yds/100m per skein): 3 skeins #0059 black; 1 skein #0047 red (CC1)

〔4〕 Ístex *Léttlopi* (100% pure Icelandic wool, 1.75oz/50g, 109yds/100m per skein): scrap lengths in the colors of your choice (CC2) or see chart for suggestions

Size 6, 9, and 10½ (4, 5.5, and 7.5mm) circular needle or double-pointed needles

Pair of magnets

Metal ring for key chain

Grosgrain ribbon about 1 ½"/4cm wide and 63"/160 cm long

Piece of sturdy plastic sheet about 1 ½"/4cm wide and 9 ½"/24cm long

Embroidery needle

Sewing needle

GAUGE
14 sts and 19 rows = 4"/10cm in St st using size 9 (5mm) needle

12 sts and 14 rows = 4"/10cm in St st using size 10½–11 (7.5mm) needle

Adjust needle size as necessary to obtain gauge.

Instructions

Bottom

With CC and size 10½–11 (7.5mm) needle, CO 12 sts. Join, taking care not to twist sts, pm EOR (end of rnd). Work in St st for 34 rnds (9½"/24cm), adapt needle size as necessary. BO.

Flattened, the tube makes a double-layered rectangle inside which the piece of plastic sheet will be inserted later.

Body

With MC and size 9 (5.5mm) needle, pick up and k34 sts along the length of the rectangle (go under two legs of each st), 6 sts along the width (catch the two layers of the tube opening together), 34 sts from the other length, 6 sts along the other width (catch only the lower layer of the tube, in order to keep the tube opened from the inside of the bag), pm EOR—80 sts.

Knit around in St st for about 14"/36.5cm.

Mark the handles as follows: k5, *knit next 6 sts with contrasting scrap yarn, place sts on left needle and knit them again with main color, k12, k6 next sts with contrasting scrap yarn, place sts on left needle and knit them again with MC,* knit next 16 sts, rep between * and *, knit rem 11 sts.

Cont knitting straight for 4"/10cm from handles (folding edge).

BO 6 sts, knit next 22 sts, and BO rem sts. Set live 22 sts aside.

Pocket

With CC1 and US 9 (5.5mm) needle, CO 22 sts.

Keeping continuity, purl the 22 sts that were set aside from the WS—44 sts. Join in the rnd, pm EOR. Work 4 rnds in garter st (*knit 1 rnd, purl 1 rnd* twice), then cont in St st until pocket is 7"/18cm long. Divide sts on 2 needles and BO using 3-needle method.

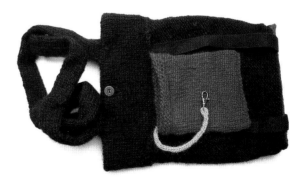

Handles

Remove scrap yarn and place sts on needle; pick up an extra st on each of the outer corners of the handle hole and k2tog with next st in next rnd—12 sts. Pm EOR. Knit in the rnd for 15"/38cm. Set live sts aside on spare needle. Do the same for each of the four handles, and then graft the first two and the last two together, being careful not to twist.

Key Chain

With any CC2 color and using size US 4 (3.5mm) needle, CO 3 sts. Work an I-cord for about 6"/15cm. BO.

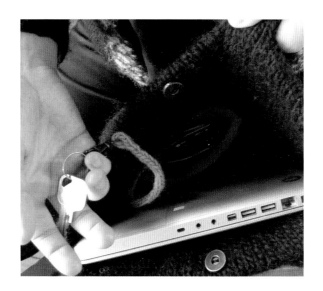

Finishing

Weave in loose ends. Insert the piece of plastic sheet inside the tube at the bottom (inside the bag) and close the opening.

The grosgrain ribbon runs inside the handles and around the bag from the inside to avoid the knit fabric from distorting with heavy objects. Attach a safety pin to one end of the grosgrain ribbon and draw it inside one handle, being careful not to twist it, wrap it around the bottom of the bag, then draw it inside the 2nd handle. Wrap it around the bottom of the bag and sew both ends together. Secure the ribbon in place, especially at the bottom of the bag, with a few sts. Fold the top edge inside the bag and sew it down. Sew the pocket down inside the bag. Be careful that the sewing doesn't show on the RS. Sew one end of the key chain inside the pocket, just below the opening at a corner, and attach a metal ring at the other side. Sew the magnets inside the bag between the handles, about ½"/1cm from edge, facing. You may also choose to line the bag.

With CC2, embroider pattern A2 in the middle of one face. Position the center of the embroidery at the center of the bag; work your way down and up the centerline of motif, then out from center.

Tip: Insert a newspaper inside the bag to make sure you don't catch both layers of fabric while sewing.

SKAGAFJÖRÐUR TOTE BAG CHART A2

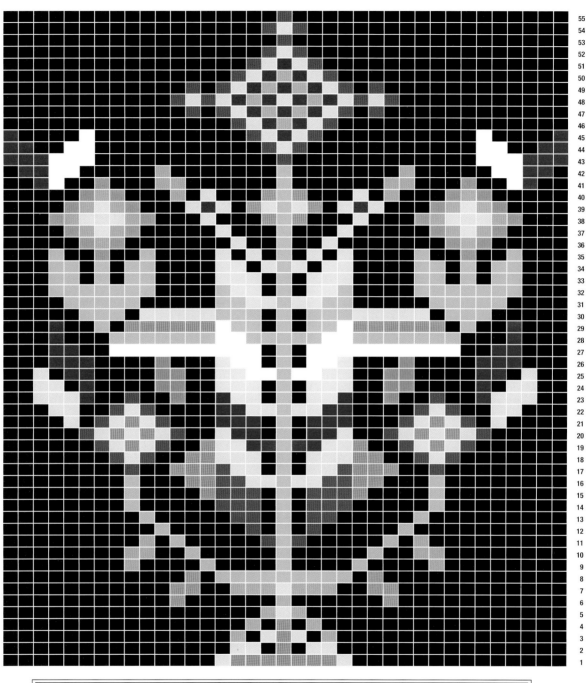

KEY

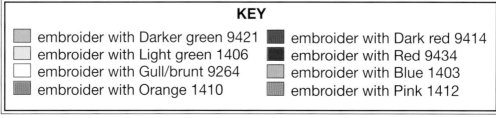

- embroider with Darker green 9421
- embroider with Light green 1406
- embroider with Gull/brunt 9264
- embroider with Orange 1410
- embroider with Dark red 9414
- embroider with Red 9434
- embroider with Blue 1403
- embroider with Pink 1412

MÖTULL CAPELET

The *Mötull* is a cape made of woolen fabric, usually flannel but sometimes silk. The length varied with time, but it often reached the mid-calf. Sigurður Guðmundsson made a shorter version to go with the *Skautbúningur* and even drew a special motif to decorate it. My version is more like a capelet, and I used a leaf pattern similar to my *Skautbúningur* sweater.

SIZES
Women's X-small (small, medium, large), 1X, 2X, 3X

FINISHED MEASUREMENTS
At lower edge: 4 ½ (47, 50 ½ , 54), 58, 61, 69"/115.5
(119.5, 128.5, 137), 147.5, 155, 175.5cm at the lower
edge

Around neck: 15 (15, 18½ 18 ½), 22, 22, 25¾"/38 (38, 47,
47), 56, 56, 65.5cm

Height: 15¾ (15¾, 16½, 16½), 17, 18, 18"/ 40 (40, 42, 42),
43, 45.5, 45.5cm

MATERIALS 5
Ístex *Álafosslopi* (100% pure Icelandic wool, 3.5oz
/100g, 109yds/100m per skein): 4 (4, 4, 4), 5, 5, 5
skeins #0484 green (MC); 2 skeins #0059 black (CC)

Size 15 (10mm) circular needle

3 pairs of black eyes and hooks

Darning needle

GAUGE
9 sts and 12 rows = 4"/10 cm in St st using size 15
(10mm) needle yarn held double

*Adjust needle size as necessary to obtain correct
gauge.*

Instructions
With MC held double and size US 15 (10mm) needle,
CO 90 (98, 106, 114), 122, 130, 138 sts. Work in
garter st for 6 rows.

Following chart, work stranded motif in St st
according to sizes with a 4-st garter st border on
each side.

Note that each square represents 2 sts and 2 rows.

Row 1: K4, knit stranded charted motif, knit last 4 sts.

Row 2: K4, purl stranded charted motif, knit last 4 sts.

Rep these 2 rows until motif is complete, then begin
working decs according to sizes beginning with Row
13 (11, 9, 7), 5, 3, 1 and ending at Row 25 (25, 23,
23), 21, 21, 19 (RS).

INSPIRED BY
This *Skautbúningur* costume was made by Kristín Jónsdóttir
(1850–1937) probably in 1870. It was given to the museum
by her great granddaughters, the daughters of Kristín
Sigurdardóttir—who was named after her grandmother—to
honor her memory. The green cape, or *mötull*, has big
appliqué flannel black leaves, outlined with a golden thread.
The Textile Museum in Blönduós.

Row 1: K4, *k13, ssk* 4 times, k10, *k2tog, k13* 4 times, k4.

Row 2 and all even rows: K4, purl to 4 sts before EOR, k4.

Row 3: K4, *k12, ssk* 4 times, k10, *k2tog, k12* 4 times, k4.

Row 5: K4, *k11, ssk* 4 times, k10, *k2tog, k11* 4 times, k4.

Row 7: K4, *k10, ssk* 4 times, k10, *k2tog, k10* 4 times, k4.

Row 9: K4, *k9, ssk* 4 times, k10, *k2tog, k9* 4 times, k4.

Row 11: K4, *k8, ssk* 4 times, k10, *k2tog, k8* 4 times, k4.

Row 13: K4, *k7, ssk* 4 times, k10, *k2tog, k7* 4 times, k4.

Row 15: K4, *k6, ssk* 4 times, k10, *k2tog, k6* 4 times, k4.

Row 17: K4, *k5, ssk* 4 times, k10, *k2tog, k5* 4 times, k4.

Row 19: K4, *k4, ssk* 4 times, k10, *k2tog, k4* 4 times, k4.

Row 21: K4, *k3, ssk* 4 times, k10, *k2tog, k3* 4 times, k4.

Row 23: K4, *k2, ssk* 4 times, k10, *k2tog, k2* 4 times, k4.

Row 25: K4, *k1, ssk* 4 times, k10, *k2tog, k1* 4 times, k4.

Work 6 rows in garter st (knit all rows) on rem 34 (34, 42, 42), 50, 50, 58 sts.

Next row (WS): BO loosely: K1, *k1, insert left needle through the 2 sts and k2tog through the back loops* to EOR (end of row).

Finishing

Darn in all ends. Hand wash in lukewarm water with wool soap. Squeeze excess water and lay flat to dry. Sew on eyes and hooks, facing each other, with about 4"/10cm between.

MÖTULL CAPELET CHART

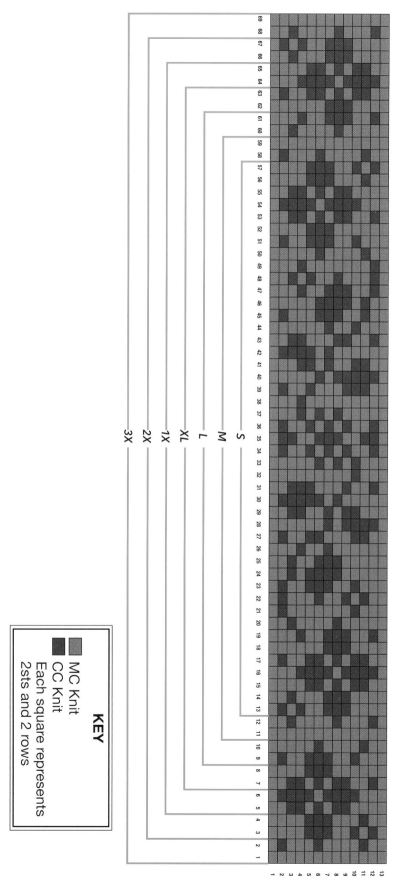

KEY

MC Knit
CC Knit
Each square represents
2 sts and 2 rows

NORDIC KNITS

THE MISSING LOPI SWEATER

The so-called *lopapeysa*—literally "made with lopi sweater," with its recognizable yoke patterning—is probably the most prominent representation of Icelandic knitting today. But you won't find any in the Textile Museum nor in other Icelandic museums because this "traditional" sweater is actually fairly new. In the 1950s, yoke sweaters became fashionable in the Western world. Nobody really knows how and when exactly the first *lopapeysa* came to be, but there are a few Icelandic women who claim to have knitted the first. What is certain is that by the 1970s, the *lopapeysa* had become so popular that it was probably one of the most sought-after sweaters in the world. The first yoke patterns were made of geometrical motifs with decreases between the motif bands. Then women began to include decreases within the motif and started to invent or adapt countless motifs, seeking inspiration in Icelandic nature, paintings, and old pattern manuscripts. Even today, one could say the *lopapeysa* is in constant state of evolution.

My design is for a rather fitted sweater that remains fairly traditional in shape, with the exception of a few short rows that I added to lift the back and lower the front, creating a more natural neckline.

SIZES
Men's small (medium, large 1X), 2X, 3X, 4X

FINISHED MEASUREMENTS
Bust: 35 (39, 42, 47), 49, 54, 57"/89 (99, 106.5, 119.5), 124.5, 137, 145cm

Body length to underarm: 16 (16½, 17, 17½), 18, 18, 18½"/ 40.5 (42, 43, 44.5), 45.5, 45.5, 47cm

Sleeve length to underarm: 19 (19½, 20, 20½), 21, 21, 21½"/ 48.5 (49.5, 51, 52), 53.5, 53.5, 54.5cm

MATERIALS ▩4▩

Ístex *Léttlopi* (100% pure Icelandic wool, 1.75oz/50g, 109yds/100m per skein): 10 (10, 10, 11), 11, 12, 12 skeins #9420 navy (MC); 2 (2, 2, 2), 2, 3, 3 skeins #0053 acorn (CC)

Sizes 6 and 7 (4 and 4.5mm) circular needle

Magic loop is used for smaller diameters or double-pointed needles

Stitch markers

Darning needle

GAUGE

18 sts and 24 rows = 4"/10cm in St st using size 7 (4.5mm) needle

Adjust needle size as necessary to obtain correct gauge.

Instructions

Sleeves

With CC and size 6 (4mm) circular needle, CO 42 (44, 46, 48), 50, 52, 54 sts. Join, taking care not to twist sts, pm EOR (end of rnd), change to MC and work rib in *k1, p1* for 2"/5cm.

Change to size 7 (4.5mm) circular needle.

Work around in St st, inc 1 st after first st and 1 st before last st every 9 (9, 9, 9), 8, 8, 8 rnds 12 (12, 12, 12), 13, 13, 13 times:

K1, M1, knit to 1 st before EOR, M1, knit rem st.

Cont even in St st on 66 (68, 70, 72), 76, 78, 80 sts until sleeve measures 19 (19½, 20, 20½), 21, 21, 21½"/48.5 (49.5, 51, 52), 53.5, 53.5, 54.5cm or when reaching desired length.

Knit to 5 (5, 6, 6), 6, 7, 7 sts before EOR and place next 10 (10, 10, 12), 12, 14, 14 underarm sts on a st holder—56 (58, 60, 60), 64, 64, 66 sts. Break off yarn, leaving enough tail to later graft the underarms. Set sleeve aside and knit the other sleeve the same way.

Body

With MC and size 6 (4mm) circular needle, CO 158 (174, 188, 210), 220, 242, 256 sts. Join, taking care not to twist sts, pm EOR, and work in rib in *k1, p1* for 2"/5cm.

Change to size 7 (4.5mm) circular needle.

Work around in St st until body measures 16 (16½, 17, 17½), 18, 18, 18½"/40.5 (42, 43, 44.5), 45.5, 45.5, 47cm.

Yoke

Combine body and sleeves on size 7 (4.5mm) circular needle (EOR is at the juncture between back and left sleeve):

With MC yarn from the body, join in and k56 (58, 60, 60), 64, 64, 66 sts of left sleeve, set next 10 (10, 10, 12), 12, 14, 14 sts of the body on a st holder (underarm sts), knit next 70 (77, 84, 93), 98, 107, 114 body front sts, knit 56 (58, 60, 60), 64, 64, 66 sts of right sleeve, set next 10 (10, 10, 12), 12, 14, 14 sts of body on a st holder (underarm sts), knit rem 70 (77, 84, 93), 98, 107,

114 body back sts—252 (270, 288, 306), 324, 342, 360 sts.

Knit 1 rnd.

Short Rows

Work back and shoulders longer with short rows to lower the neckline at the front:

K73 (77, 81, 83), 88, 90, 94, turn, yo, purl back on 216 (231, 246, 259), 274, 287, 302 sts [which means purl to 36 (39, 42, 47), 50, 55, 58 sts before gap] turn, yo, *knit to 3 sts (2 sts and the yo) before gap, turn, yo, purl to 3 sts before gap, turn, yo* repeat from * to * 3 times; cont to knit in the rnd to EOR.

Next Rnd: Close gaps (see also Technique on page 187):

Knit the first 4 yo's with the next st as k2tog and the 4 last yo's with the st before as ssk.

Yoke Pattern

Follow chart until Rnd 42 has been completed—70 (75, 80, 85), 90, 95, 100 sts rem.

Cont with MC and dec 0 (1, 4, 7), 10, 13, 16 sts on rnd as follows:

Size M: Dec 1 st anywhere in the rnd.

Size L: *K18, k2tog* 4 times.

Size 1X: *K10, k2tog* 7 times, knit rem st.

Size 2X: *K7, k2tog* 9 times.

Size 3X: *K5, k2tog* 13 times, k4 rem sts.

Size 4X: *k4, k2tog* 16 times, k4 rem sts.

70 (74, 76, 78), 80, 82, 84 sts rem.

Work 4 rnds in *k1, p1* rib. BO loosely in rib pattern:

Work 1 st, *work 1 st, insert left needle in the 2 sts on right needle and work them together* across.

Finishing

Graft underarm sts and darn in all ends.

Hand wash the sweater delicately in lukewarm water with gentle wool soap. Leave flat to dry.

MISSING LOPI SCHEMATIC

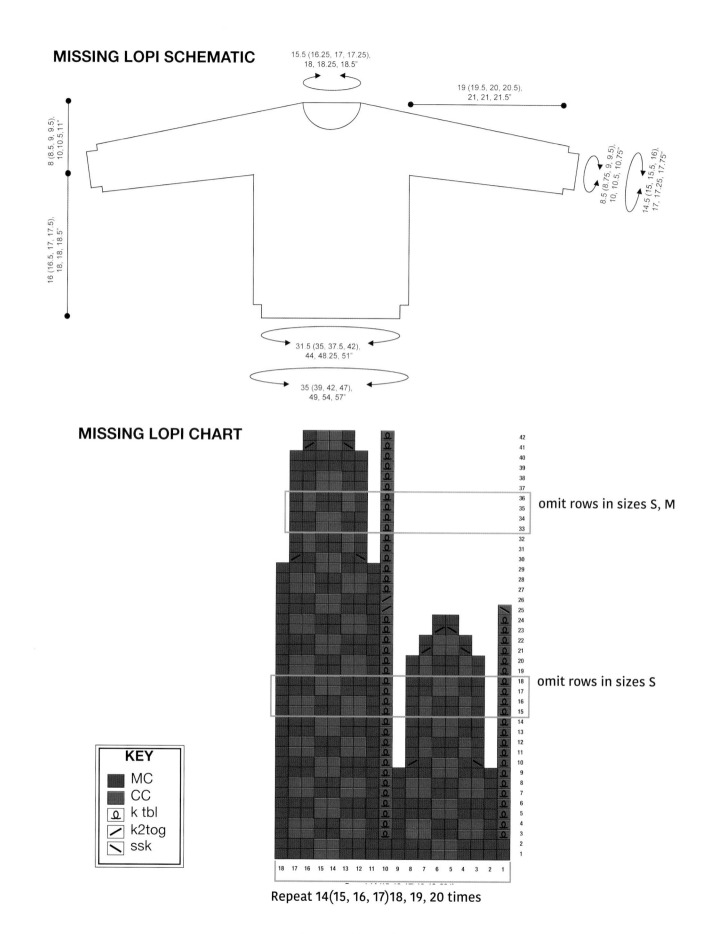

15.5 (16.25, 17, 17.25,
18, 18.25, 18.5"

19 (19.5, 20, 20.5),
21, 21, 21.5"

8 (8.5, 9, 9.5),
10, 10.5, 11"

8.5 (8.75, 9, 9.5),
10, 10.5, 10.75"

14.5 (15, 15.5, 16),
17, 17.25, 17.75"

16 (16.5, 17, 17.5),
18, 18, 18.5"

31.5 (35, 37.5, 42),
44, 48.25, 51"

35 (39, 42, 47),
49, 54, 57"

MISSING LOPI CHART

omit rows in sizes S, M

omit rows in sizes S

KEY

- ▇ MC
- ▇ CC
- ⨀ k tbl
- ╱ k2tog
- ╲ ssk

Repeat 14(15, 16, 17)18, 19, 20 times

ICELANDIC SHOE INSERTS

Many inserts were knitted in Icelandic intarsia, intarsia made using garter stitch. The tradition is unique to Iceland and was used to knit mostly shoe inserts. In fact, the technique is called *rósaleppaprjón*, literally meaning "rose-pattern insert knitting." It was most common to knit inserts in three pieces using garter stitch to ensure the inserts would retain their shape. An insert knitted in one piece tends to stretch and become too long. The middle section is knitted first, and then stitches are picked up at the edge and the tips knitted. There were no knitting patterns for inserts, nor specific instructions, because the inserts had to be tailored to fit the person for whom they were made and adjusted to accommodate the type of yarn used, among other things. Please feel free to adapt this basic shoe insert pattern to any yarn, needle size, or foot.

SIZE
Women's shoe size US 7–9 (EU 36–40)

FINISHED MEASUREMENTS
Width: 4¼"/11cm

Length: 9½"/24cm

Note: You can achieve more sizes by changing yarn/
needle size or adding/removing rows/stitches.

MATERIALS 🧶0
Ístex *Einband-Loðband* (70% Icelandic wool, 30%
wool, 1¾ oz/50gr, 246yds/225m per skein): 1 skein
color of choice (MC); remnants in the colors of your
choice (CC),

Size 0/2mm double-pointed needles

Sizes C-2/2.75mm crochet hooks

Darning needle

GAUGE
32 sts and 64 rows = 4"/10cm in garter st using size 0
(2mm) needle

*Adjust needle size as necessary to obtain correct
gauge.*

Note: In the intarsia motif, each square represents
1 st and 2 rows (= 1 garter ridge).

Pattern Notes

Inserts are often knitted in garter stitch in one piece from heel to toe or in three stages: First the rectangle middle piece is knitted, then stitches are picked up at the selvedge on both sides and the tips worked. An Icelandic intarsia motif is positioned in the center of the foot. Tips are often decorated with stripes or a smaller intarsia motif, especially in the inserts knitted in three stages.

Instructions

Inserts knitted in one piece from heel to toe. (Make two the same.)

With MC, CO 4 sts.

Knit 2 rows in garter st.

Following chart of choice, inc 1 st on both sides 14 times: kfb at the beginning of each row until there are 32 sts.

Knit 116 rows (= 58 garter ridges).

Dec 1 st on both sides 14 times: k2tog at the beginning of each row until 4 sts rem. BO.

Inserts knitted in three stages. (Make two the same.)

With MC, CO 46 sts.

Stage #1:

Following chart of choice, knit 64 rows (= 32 garter ridges) and BO.

Stages #2 and #3:

Pick up 32 sts from the selvedge (between each garter st ridge) and work 12 rows (6 garter ridges).

Cont to follow chosen chart, dec 1 st on both sides 14 times: K2tog at the beginning of each row until 4 sts rem. BO.

Work the 2nd tip the same way, picking up sts on the other selvedge.

Finishing

With a CC, crochet an edge of sc around the insert. Hand wash with wool soap and slightly felt by rubbing. Leave flat to dry.

INSPIRED BY

Here are a few shoe insert samples from the large collection at the Textile Museum. All were used inside the shoes except for the one on the right. It was knit with horsehair and was used between the shoe and an outer leather sock—the boot of those times. You would therefore wear two pairs of inserts at once.

ICELANDIC SHOE INSERT CHARTS

Chart A: Stripes

Chart B: Diamond Rose

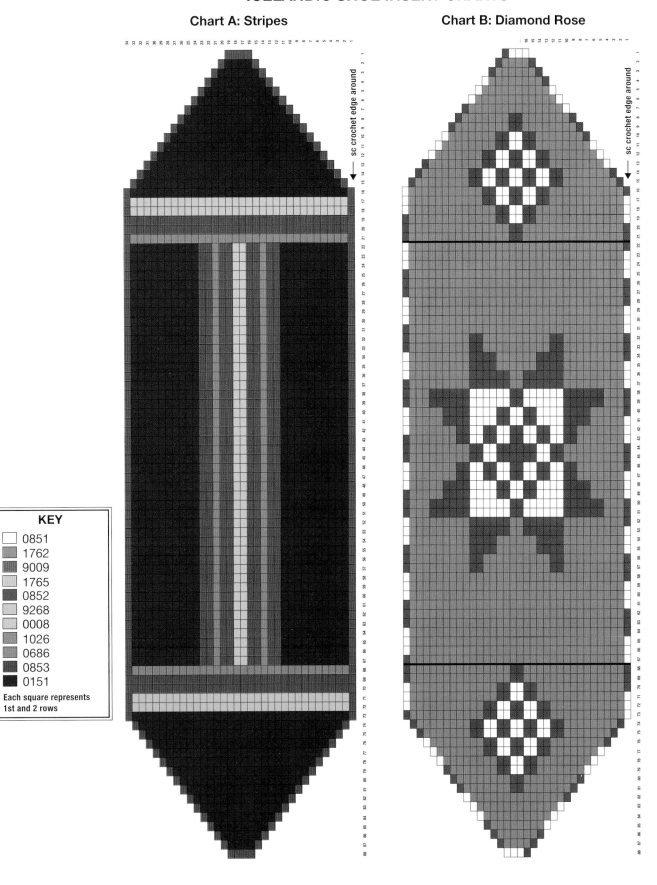

KEY

☐	0851
▨	1762
▨	9009
▨	1765
■	0852
▨	9268
▨	0008
▨	1026
▨	0686
▨	0853
■	0151

Each square represents
1st and 2 rows

Chart C: Flower Pot

Chart D: Windrose

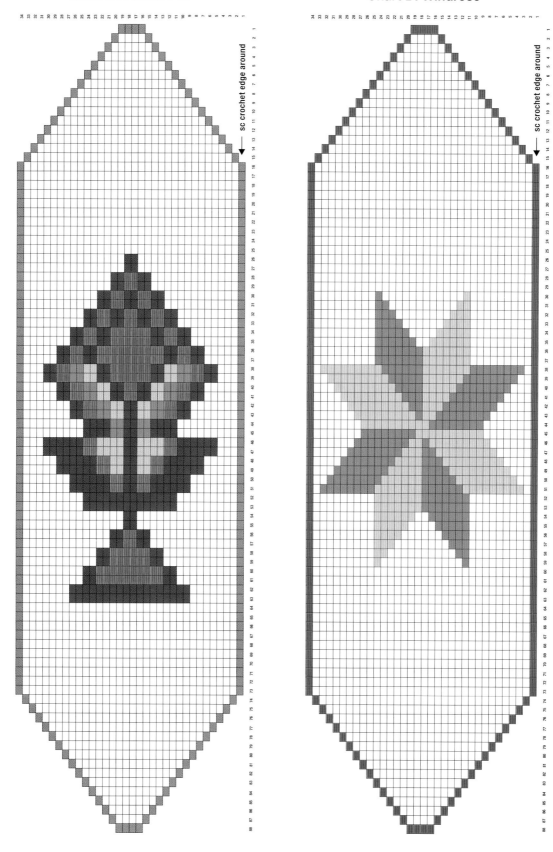

NORDIC KNITS

ICELANDIC SOFT SHOES

I couldn't help but design a knitted soft shoe to go with the shoe inserts. As a matter of fact, there are a few knitted slippers in the Textile Museum, but I wanted mine to replicate the traditional skin shoes. I more or less kept the proportions of the cut leather, but made use of clever shaping to avoid the sewing that is normally involved in such shoes. Instead of the string that was often braided around the foot to prevent the shoes from falling off, I added a crocheted strap with a little button. And mind you, with a knitted insert inside, these shoes are the most comfortable and warm slippers I have ever worn!

SIZES
One size fits all, adjustable in length where indicated
  in instructions

FINISHED MEASUREMENTS
Length: 10"/25.5cm

Height: 3"/7.5cm

MATERIALS 5
Ístex *Álafosslopi* (100% pure Icelandic wool,
  3.5oz/100g, 109yds/100m per skein): 1 skein #0005
  black heather (MC); less than .20oz/5g #0051
  white (CC)

Size 8 (5mm) circular needle (or double-pointed
  needles)

Size G-6 (4mm) crochet hook

Stitch marker

Darning needle

GAUGE
14 sts and 21 rows = 4"/10cm in St st using size 8
  (5mm) needles

Adjust needle size as necessary to obtain gauge.

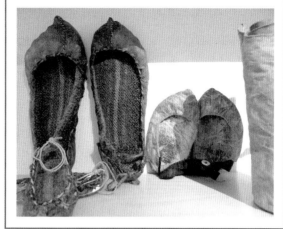

Instructions

With a provisional cast-on, CO 20 sts with MC and size 8 (5mm) needle, leaving a 12"/30cm tail (later used to graft heel sts).

Work back and forth in St st:

Row 1: Knit all sts.

Row 2 and all even rows: Purl all sts.

Row 3: K9, M1, k2, M1, k9—22 sts.

Row 5: K10, M1, k2, M1, k10—24 sts.

Row 7: K11, M1, k2, M1, k11—26 sts.

Row 9: K12, M1, k2, M1, k12—28 sts.

Row 11: Knit all sts.

Row 13: K2, k2tog, k2, k2tog, k12 , ssk, k2, ssk, k2—24 sts. Mark this row.

Cont even for 4"/10cm from marked row (this is for a foot length of 10"/25.5cm) or desired length (to decrease or increase sizes, add or deduct 1"/ 2.5cm per size).

Join in the rnd. Knit 1 rnd, pm EOR (end of rnd).

Inc in next rnd: K2, *M1, k1* 4 times, knit to 3 sts before EOR, *M1, k1* 4 times, k1—32 sts.

Work 1 rnd.

Dec in every rnd: *Knit to 6 sts before EOR, ssk, k2, k2tog* until 4 sts rem on needle.

Break off yarn and draw it through the sts.

Remove provisional cast-on, set live sts on needle, fold in two, and graft heel.

Finishing

With CC, crochet an edging of sc around: 1 sl st at the back of the shoe, 2 ch (count as a sc), 1 sc in every other st. Add a strap 3½"/9 cm from back (on left side for right shoe and on right side for left shoe): Ch 20, sl 5 extra ch to make a loop, then crochet back to edge (1 sc in each ch), cont working sc edging to EOR, join rnd with a sl st in top chain.

STEP ROSE CUSHION

Although most inserts were knitted in Icelandic intarsia, examples of other artifacts using the technique do exist. I reinterpreted the flat seat cushion into a big cuddly cushion. The center rose is knitted in Icelandic intarsia, but the two colorful crosses in each rose are later embroidered in the same manner, as some inserts from the Textile Museum were. It makes the intarsia work extremely easy, with only three blocks of color across the row.

FINISHED MEASUREMENTS
16"/40.5cm square

MATERIALS 4
Ístex *Léttlopi* (100% pure Icelandic wool, 1.75oz/50g, 109yds/100m per skein): 2 skeins #0059 black (MC); 1 skein and 10g #1411 yellow (CC1); 1 skein #1418 chair (CC2); 10g each #1402 blue (CC3), 10g #9434 red (CC4)

Size 4 (3.5mm) needles

Cushion to fit dimensions

Darning needle

GAUGE
20 sts and 40 rows = 4"/10cm in St st with 4 rows in garter st using size 4 (3.5mm) needle

Adjust needle size as necessary to obtain correct gauge.

INSPIRED BY
The motif on these inserts is not worked in Icelandic intarsia but embroidered with start cross-stitches. The Textile Museum in Blönduós.

Instructions

With MC, CO 82 sts.

Note: Each square in the chart pattern represents 2 sts and 4 rows in garter stitch.

Following chart, work pattern in Icelandic intarsia (intarsia in garter stitch) with colorway A (front cover).

Keeping the continuity, work pattern again, but with colorway B (back cover). BO.

Finishing

Secure ends inside the cushion (you don't necessarily have to darn them in).

Embroider the two crosses on each rose with a star st.

Fold cushion cover in two, sew sides with a flat seam leaving a hole big enough at the bottom. Insert cushion and sew down the hole.

STEP ROSE CUSHION CHART

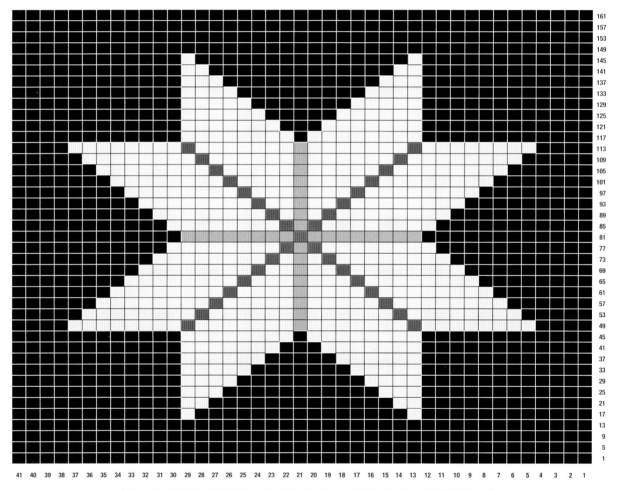

KEY

Colorway A	Colorway B
K MC	K MC
K CC1	K CC2
K CC1, embroider with CC3	K CC2, embroider with CC1
K CC1, embroider with CC4	K CC2, embroider with CC2

Each square is 2 sts and 4 rows.

BROKEN ROSE BLANKET

I reinterpreted the broken rose frame in the Textile Museum as a blanket but used intarsia in stockinette stitch instead of the Icelandic intarsia in garter stitch. The simple border in garter stitch is reminiscent of the original technique. The color combination is similar to the original colorway but with a light background, giving it a very soft look that's more suitable for a baby.

FINISHED MEASUREMENTS
31 by 41"/78.5 by 104cm

MATERIALS 🧶5️⃣
Ístex *Álafosslopi* (100% pure Icelandic wool, 3.5oz/100g, 109yds/100m per skein): 7 skeins #0051 white (MC); 1 skein #9972 ecru heather (CC1); 2 skeins #9973 wheat heather (CC2); 3 skeins #9984 fairy green (CC3); 1 skein #9983 apple green (CC4); 2 skeins #0008 light denim heather (CC5)

Size 10½ (6.5mm) needles (for intarsia band) and circular needle (for border)

Note: Working intarsia with a circular needle is not recommended.

Cushion to dimensions

Stitch markers

Darning needle

GAUGE
14 sts and 17 rows = 4"/10cm in St st

Gauge not essential.

INSPIRED BY
This piece of knitting is stretched on a wooden frame with pins and is about 22 by 22" (56 x 56cm). It is knitted very loose in Icelandic intarsia (garter stitch). The motif represents a *þríbrotin áttabladarós*, literally a three broken eight-petal rose that, according to Elsa E. Guðjónsson, seems to be a motif unique to Iceland. It is, however, a common motif in Icelandic handwork, and you can find it charted in the Skaftatfell pattern manuscript book from the eighteenth century. The Textile Museum in Blönduós, Reference HB33.

NORDIC KNITS

Instructions

With a provisional cast-on, using MC and size 10½ (6.5mm) needle, CO 122 sts.

Following Chart, work motif in intarsia.

When motif is complete, knit a garter st border around:

Cont with MC and circ needle: Knit across, pm, pick up 1 st at the corner, pm, pick up 80 sts along the edge (about 2 sts out of 3), pm, pick up 1 st at the corner, pm, remove provisional cast-on and k122 live sts, pm, pick up 1 st at the corner, pm, pick up 80 sts along the other edge, pm, pick up 1 st at the corner, pm EOR (end of rnd)—408 sts.

Work in garter st and inc (with yo) 1 st on both sides of corner sts in every other rnd:

Rnd 1: Purl all sts.

Rnd 2: *Knit to marker, yo on right side of it, k1 (corner st), yo on left side of next marker* 4 times, knit rem sts to EOR.

Repeat these 2 rnds 3 times—432 sts.

BO as follows: P1, *place st back on left needle, p2tog* across.

Break off yarn and pull it through.

Finishing

Darn in all ends. Hand wash in lukewarm water with wool soap. Squeeze excess water and lay flat to dry.

BROKEN ROSE BLANKET CHART

KEY

☐	K 0051 MC
☐	K 9972 CC1
▨	K 9973 CC2
☐	K 9984 CC3
▨	K 9983 CC4
☐	K 0008 CC5

Each square represents
2 sts and 2 rows

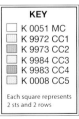

TOGARA SOCKS

The original socks that inspired this pattern were intended for mass production, so my pattern includes many sizes to fit everyone in the family. I used Hosuband, which is an Icelandic wool blended with nylon—an extremely hard-wearing blend that is suitable for socks. Hand-knitted knee socks tend to fall down to the ankles, which is why bands used to be braided in the tops of socks to hold them up. These days, elastic has taken the place of the braids. Rather than using elastic in my socks, the cuff is tubular with a little buttonhole through which you can draw a woven band or a nice ribbon. You can change the ribbon as often as you like for dramatically different effects. I like how the rather rough socks take on a feminine feel when laced with a delicate, transparent ribbon with golden threads.

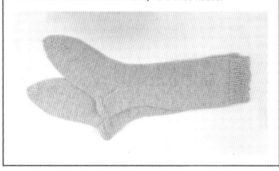

SIZES

XS (S, M, L), XL for Child (Teen, Women, Women/Men) Men

Finished Measurements

Circumference: 6 (7, 8, 9), 9¾"/15 (18, 20.5, 23), 25cm

Length: 6 (8, 10, 11), 11½"/15 (20.5, 25.5, 28), 29cm

MATERIALS 🧶4

stex *Hosuband* (80% new wool, 20% polyamide, 3.5oz/100g, 142yds/130m per skein): 2 skeins #0005 light gray

Sizes 6 and 7 (4 and 4.5mm) circular needles

(Magical loop is used for smaller diameters or double-pointed needles.)

Stitch markers

Darning needle

Thread and needle

Fancy ribbon about 72"/183cm long and 1"/2.5cm wide

GAUGE

18 sts and 22 rows = 4"/10cm in St st using size 7 (4.5mm) needle

Adjust needle size as necessary to obtain gauge.

Instructions
Cuff

With a provisional cast-on, using size 6 (4mm) circular needle, CO 30 (34, 38, 42), 46 sts. Join, taking care not to twist sts, pm EOR (end of rnd).

Work in St st for 6 rnds.

Work in *k1, p1* rib for 6 rnds, making a buttonhole in the 3rd rnd:

Left sock: K7 (8, 9, 10), 11, BO 3 sts in rib pattern (CO 3 sts over BO sts in next rnd).

Right sock: K20 (23, 26, 29), 32, BO 3 sts in rib pattern (CO 3 sts over BO sts in next rnd).

Remove provisional cast-on, place sts on spare needle, fold cuff in two (rib facing, reverse St st inside the sock), and work the sts from each needle together—30 (34, 38, 42), 46 sts.

Alternatively, omit provisional cast-on, CO normally, fold cuff in two and sew down on the inside.

Leg

Change to size 7 (4.5mm) needle. Work in St st for about 4 (6, 7 ½, 8 ¼), 9"/10 (15, 19, 21), 23cm or 4"/10cm short of ankle bone, inc 4 sts evenly spaced in first rnd:

K7 (8, 9, 10), 11, M1 4 times, knit rem sts—34 (38, 42, 46), 50 sts.

Dec at ankle:

Rnd 1: K1, k2tog, knit to 3 sts before EOR, ssk, knit rem st.

Rnds 2-6: Knit all sts.

Repeat these 6 rnds 3 times in all—28 (32, 36, 40), 44 sts.

Work 4 more rnds.

Heel Flap

Next rnd: K7 (8, 9, 10), 11, turn and work 14 (16, 18, 20), 22 sts back and forth in St st for 10 (12, 14, 16), 18 rows. Always slip first st in row; end with a knit row (RS).

Heel Turn

Row 1 (WS): P9 (10, 11, 12), 13, p2tog, turn.

Row 2: Sl 1 pwise, k4, ssk, turn.

Row 3: Sl 1 pwise wyif, p4, p2tog, turn.

Rep Rows 2 and 3 until 6 sts rem, ending on a RS row.

Cont working in the rnd.

Gusset

Rnd 1: Pick up and k5 (6, 7, 8), 9 sts along the edge of the heel flap, M1 at the gap (make a double lifted dec, see Technique on page 133), pm, knit across instep, pm, M1 at the gap, pick up and k5 (6, 7, 8), 9 sts along the other edge of the heel flap, knit to EOR (center back)—32 (36, 40, 44), 48 sts.

Rnd 2: K7 (8, 9, 10), 11, ssk, k14 (16, 18, 20), 22, k2tog, knit to EOR—30 (34, 38, 42), 46 sts.

Rnd 3: Knit all sts.

Rnd 4: K6 (7, 8, 9), 10, ssk, k14 (16, 18, 20), 22, k2tog, knit to EOR—28 (32, 36, 40), 44 sts.

Foot

Work 8 (9, 10, 11), 12 rnds even in St st.

Instep-short-row rnd: K21 (24, 27, 30), 33, turn, yo, p14 (16, 18, 20), 22 sts, turn, yo.

Cont knitting in the rnd: Knit to first yo, k2tog (yo and next st), knit to EOR.

Next rnd: Knit to 1 st before yo, ssk (st and yo), knit to EOR.

Work 7 (8, 9, 10), 11 rnds, then rep Instep-short-row rnd and Next rnd.

Work even until foot measures 4 (5½, 7, 7¾), 7¾"/10 (14, 18, 19.5), 19.5cm or about 2 (2½, 3, 3¼), 3¾"/5 (6.5, 7.5, 8.5), 9.5cm short of tip of the toe.

Toe

Place side markers: K7 (8, 9, 10), 11, pm, k14 (16, 18, 20), 22, pm, knit to EOR.

Rnd 1: *Knit to 3 sts before m, ssk, k2, k2tog* twice, knit to EOR.

Rnd 2: Knit all sts.

Rep Rnds 1 and 2 until 8 sts rem on needle.

Graft back to front sts.

Finishing

Darn in all ends.

Cut ribbon in two. Draw it through the buttonhole at the cuff.

NORDIC KNITS

SOCK BAND SOCKS

This stranded pattern alternated with short rows gives the illusion of the woven bands that were braided around the legs to hold socks in place in the past. For a more striking effect, the socks are designed so they are not completely symmetrical. They are knitted from the cuff down with an afterthought heel, a star toe, and a few short rows under the sole for comfort.

SIZES
Adult's small (medium, large)

FINISHED MEASUREMENTS
Foot circumference: 6½ (8, 9¾)"/16.5 (20.5, 25)cm

Foot length: 9 (9½, 10¼)"/23 (24, 26)cm

Length from cuff to heel: 7"/18cm

MATERIALS 🧶1🧶
Knit Picks *Stroll Sock Yarn* (75% superwash merino wool, 25% nylon, 1.75oz/50g, 231yds/211m per ball): 1 ball each Black (MC); Bare (CC1); Fedora Dark Brown (CC2); Jack Rabbit Heather medium brown (CC3); Cork light brown (CC4)

Size 1 (2.25mm) circular needle or double-pointed needles

Stitch markers

Darning needle

GAUGE
32 sts and 48 rows = 4"/10cm in St st using size 1 (2.5mm) needle

Adjust needle size as necessary to obtain gauge.

INSPIRED BY
Þurídur Jónsdóttir from Sigurðarstödum í Bárðardal worked and weaved the bands that inspired me to create the pattern that runs around the socks. When the bands were made is not known. The Textile Museum in Blönduós, Reference HB569.

Pattern Note

You can obtain more sizes by changing the needle size, using smaller or larger needle. For example, 26 sts and 36 rows = 4"/10cm in St st using size 3 (3.25mm) needle.

Special Abbreviation

Central double dec s2sk (slip2, slip1, knit): Slip 2 together as if to knit, slip 1 as if to knit, insert left needle from back to front in the 3 sts and k3tog through the back loops.

Instructions

Cuff

With MC and size 1 (2.25mm) needle, CO 52 (64, 78) sts. Join, taking care not to twist sts, pm EOR (end of rnd).

Work in *k1, p1* rib for 6 rnds.

Cont with MC in St st for 2 rnds, inc 1 st in size M—52 (65, 78) sts.

Leg

Rnds 1–11: Work pattern band in stranded knitting with a jogless join.

Rnds 12–13: Work 1 rnd with MC, then short rows: turn, yo, p42 (49, 55), turn, yo, *knit to 5 sts (4 sts and a yo) before gap, turn, yo, purl to 5 sts before gap, turn, yo* 4 times, knit to EOR and knit next rnd closing all gaps (see Techniques).

Rnds 14–24: Work pattern band.

Rnds 25–26: Work 1 rnd with MC, then short rows: K10 (16, 23), turn, yo, p10 (16, 23), turn, yo, *knit to next yo, k2tog (yo and next st), k3, turn, yo, purl to next yo, ssp (yo and next st), p3, turn, yo* 4 times, cont to knit in the rnd, knit to next yo, k2tog, knit to 1 st before next yo, ssk, knit to EOR.

Repeat Rnds 1–26 once more.

Afterthought Heel

Cont with MC and in next rnd, work first (right foot) or last (left foot) 26 (32, 38) sts in rnd with a contrasting color scrap yarn, place sts back on left needle and knit them again with MC.

Foot

Work pattern band Rnds 1–11.

Work 3 rnds with MC, then short row across the sole: K26 (32, 38) sts (right foot) or knit to EOR (left foot), turn, yo, p26 (32, 38) sts, turn, yo. Cont knitting in the rnd, closing all gaps (see Special Techniques Used on page 187).

Work 2 more rnds with MC, then work pattern band Rnds 1–11.

Cont even with MC until foot measures 5½ (6, 6½)"/14 (15, 16.5)cm from scrap yarn or about 2"/5cm short of desired length.

Star Toe

Rnd 1: *K2tog, k11* to EOR—48 (60, 72) sts.

Rnd 2 and all even rows: Knit all sts.

Rnd 3: *K2tog, k10* to EOR—44 (55, 66) sts.

Rnd 5: *K2tog, k9* to EOR—40 (50, 60) sts.

Rnd 7: *K2tog, k8* to EOR—36 (45, 54) sts.

Rnd 9: *K2tog, k7* to EOR—32 (40, 48) sts.

Rnd 11: *K2tog, k6* to EOR—28 (35, 42) sts.

Rnd 13: *K2tog, k5* to EOR—24 (30, 36) sts.

Rnd 15: *K2tog, k4* to EOR—20 (25, 30) sts.

Rnd 17: *K2tog, k3* to EOR—16 (20, 24) sts.

Rnd 19: *K2tog, k2* to EOR—12 (15, 18) sts.

Rnd 21: *K2tog, k1* to EOR—8 (10, 12) sts.

Break yarn, draw it through the sts.

Heel

Remove scrap yarn and place live sts on needles.

Work in the rnd with MC: pick up 2 extra sts and k2tog (make a double lifted dec) on each side—54 (66, 78) sts.

Work central double dec on each side in every other row; the extra picked up st is at the center of the double dec:

Rnd 1: *Knit to 1 st before extra st, s2sk* twice.

Rnd 2: Knit all sts.

Rnd 3: *Knit to 1 st before central dec st, s2sk* twice.

Rnd 4: Knit all sts.

Repeat Rnds 3 and 4 until 18 (22, 26) sts rem. Divide sts in two and graft together back to bottom to close the heel.

Finishing

Darn in ends and block.

SOCK BAND SOCKS CHART

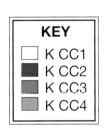

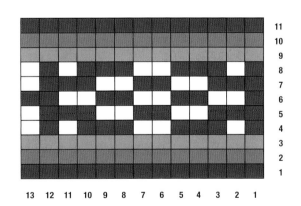

MARGRÉT TRIANGULAR SHAWL

I made very few changes to the shawl knitted by Margrét Jakobsdóttir, now in the Textile Museum, but I did add a garter tab cast-on to avoid having to sew the cast-on at the top. This design is not as fine as the original shawl, which was knitted with þel band that Margrét hand spun herself, and it has far fewer shades of gray. Margrét designed few shawls herself, but she made the first pattern for this shawl that was published in the magazine *Hugur og Hönd* in 1976, which is now out of print.

FINISHED MEASUREMENTS
Triangle at widest: 67"/170cm

Triangle height: 3½"/85cm

MATERIALS 🏵0🏵
Ístex *Einband-Loðband* (70% Icelandic wool, 30% wool, 1.75 oz/50gr 246 yds/225m per skein) 2 skeins each #0852 heather black (MC), #1026 light gray (CC3), 1 skein each #9102 dark gray (CC1), #1027 medium gray (CC2), #0851 white (CC4)

Size 6 (4mm) circular needle

Size C2 (2.75mm) crochet hook

Darning needle

GAUGE
22 sts and 26 rows = 4"/10cm in St st using size 6 (4mm) needle

Adjust needle size as necessary to obtain correct gauge.

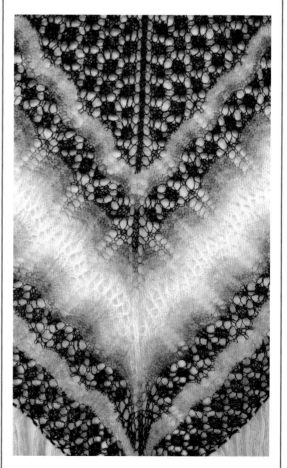

INSPIRED BY
Margrét Jakobsdóttir Lindal hand spun the þel band in natural sheep colors and used it to knit the shawl. The Textile Museum in Blönduós, Reference HIS2176.

Icelandic Handknits

Pattern Notes

Follow the charts as indicated. Only RS rows (uneven rows) are charted. WS rows (even rows) are always purled except for the first 3 and last 3 sts that are worked in garter st (borders).

The shawl is made of two identical triangles with one middle st and 3 garter st borders on both sides. The charts show only half the shawl; work the motif first from right to left, then repeat from the middle st from left to right.

Instructions

With provisional cast-on, using MC and size 6 (4mm) circular needle, CO 3 sts.

Knit 5 rows in garter st. Pick up and k3 sts along the edge of the square. Remove provisional cast-on and knit the 3 live sts—9 sts.

Rows 1–26: With MC, work Chart A Rows 1–26—71 sts at end of Row 26.

Rows 27–82: With MC, repeat Chart A Rows 19–26 seven times—239 sts at end of Row 82.

Rows 83–90: Work Chart B Rows 1–8 (repeat red frame 9 times), working Rows 1–4 with CC3 and Rows 5–8 with CC2—263 sts at end of Row 90.

Rows 91–98: With MC, work Chart A Rows 19–26—287 sts at end of Row 98.

Rows 99–134: Work Chart B Rows 1–36 (repeat red frame 11 times), working Rows 1–4 with CC1, Rows 5–8 with CC2, Rows 9–14 with CC3, Rows 15–22 with CC4, Rows 23–28 with CC3, Rows 29–32 with CC2 and Rows 33–36 with CC1—371 sts at end of Row 134.

Rows 135–142: With MC, work Chart A Rows 19–26 (repeat red frame 28 times)—395 sts.

Rows 143–150: With CC3, work chart C rows 1–8 (repeat red frame 15 times)—415 sts.

Rows 151–164: With MC, work chart D rows 1–14 (repeat red frame 32 times)—457 sts.

BO with MC and a crocheted chain bind-off: Sl st 2 together (insert hook through loops of sts as if to knit them together through the back loops, yarn over hook and pull through all sts), *ch 5, sl st 3 together* ch 5, sl st 2 last sts—152 ch arches.

Finishing

Darn in all ends, but don't cut them off yet. Hand wash in lukewarm water with wool soap. Let it soak in water for at least 20 minutes. Squeeze out excess water in a towel, pin to dimensions. Lay flat to dry. When it's dry, cut off the ends.

Fringe

Cut 12"/30.5cm lengths of CC3. Fold three strands in two and attach in each arch with the crochet hook.

CHART A

KEY

☐	k
ℓ	k tbl
O	yo
╱	k2tog (right-leaning dec)
╲	ssk (left-leaning dec)
⋏	left-leaning double dec: sl1, k2tog, psso
I	k on RS and WS (garter st borders)
☐	repeat

Column numbers (right to left): 25 23 21 19 17 15 13 11 9 7 5 3 1

Row numbers (top to bottom): 1–37

garter st border

Repeat from left to right

central sts

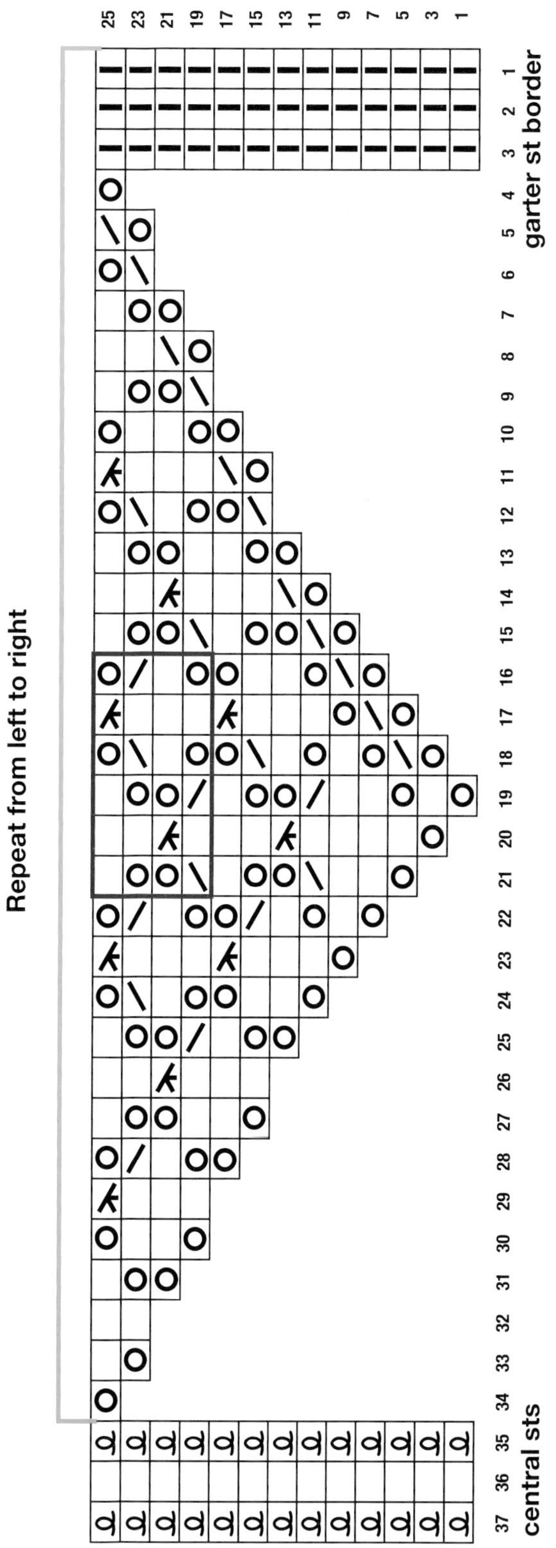

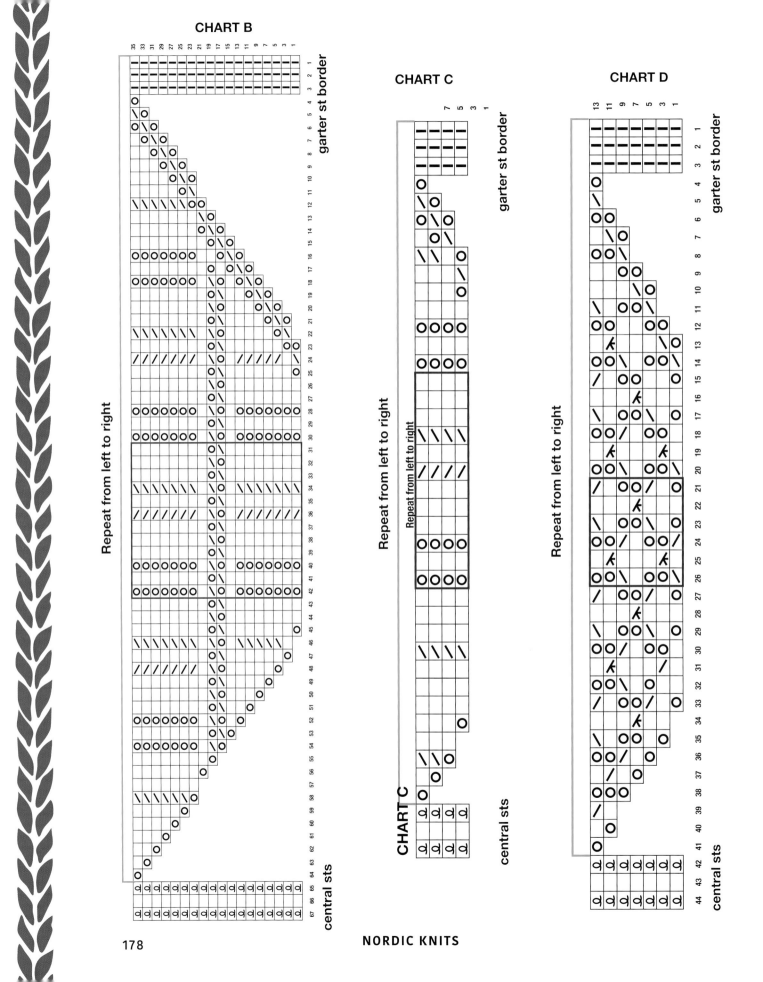

CHART B

Repeat from left to right

garter st border

central sts

CHART C

Repeat from left to right

garter st border

central sts

CHART D

Repeat from left to right

garter st border

central sts

NORDIC KNITS

KLUKKA SKIRT

This skirt is inspired by the *klukka*, the Icelandic petticoat or slip. It was worn as an undergarment, close to the skin to keep warm. It was knitted out of lightweight wool, often with a wavy lace pattern in the skirt, such as a scallop lace stitch, enhanced with a few stripes of colors and a crocheted edge. The Textile Museum has many examples of *klukka*, and several are machine knitted but finished by hand. The skirt, which is knitted from the top down, comes in many sizes and three lengths. You can easily add sizes or adjust the length. It is shaped with increases within the stitch pattern, but also by changing needle size. The shifts in shading, inspired by the lovely and subtle color shading found in shawls from the Textile Museum collection, are obtained by knitting different strands of yarn together.

SIZES
From Girl's to Women's 3X (15 sizes)

Choose size according to waist measurements (zero or negative ease)

FINISHED MEASUREMENTS
Waist: 17, 19, 21½ (23½ , 25½ , 27¾) 30, 32, 34 (36, 38½, 40½) 42½, 44¾, 47"/43, 48.5, 54.5 (59.5, 65, 70.5) 76, 81.5, 86.5 (91.5, 98, 104) 108, 113.5, 119.5cm

Height (before blocking): About 16, 16, 16 (18, 18, 18) 20, 20, 20 (22, 22, 22) 24, 24, 24"/40.5, 40.5, 40.5 (45.5, 45.5, 45.5) 51, 51, 51 (56, 56, 56) 61, 61, 61cm

Height (after blocking): Add about 1"/2.5cm

MATERIALS 3
Ístex *Plötulopi* (100% pure unspun Icelandic wool 3.5oz/100g, 228yds/200m per skein [always held doubled]): 2, 2, 2 (2, 2, 3) 3, 3, 3 (3, 4, 4) 4, 4, 4 skeins #0484 forest green (MC); 1 skein #1424 golden yellow heather (CC1); 1 skein #0059 black (CC2); 1 roving plate #0014 forest heather (CC3); 1 skein #0013 light forest heather (CC4); 1 skein #0001 white (CC5)

Sizes 7, 8, and 9 (4.5, 5, and 5.5mm) circular needles

Darning needle

Elastic for waistband, about 0.6"/1.5cm wide

GAUGE
15 sts and 21 rows = 4"/10cm in pattern st with size 7 (4.5mm) needle

Adjust needle size as necessary to obtain correct gauge.

Instructions

With MC (held doubled) and size 7 (4.5mm) circular needle, CO 64, 72, 80 (88, 96,104) 112, 120, 128 (136, 144, 152) 160, 168, 176 sts. Join, taking care not to twist sts, pm EOR (end of round).

Work around in St st for 5 rnds.

Purl 1 rnd (foldline for waistline).

Work around in St st for 7 rnds.

Following Chart, begin pattern st, repeating motif across and upward according to size and height.

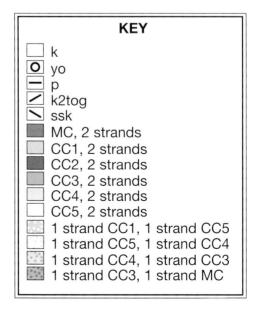

INSPIRED BY
No one knows who made the hand-knitted pink *klukka* or when. The Textile Museum in Blönduós, Reference HIS162.

Note that repeat for height (H) is indicated on the right side of the chart for first 3 sizes (2nd 3 sizes, 3rd 3 sizes, 4th 3 sizes), 5th 3 sizes.

Note: Read the chart: only uneven rnds are charted. Even rnds are always knit. The repeat rnds mean you have to repeat the pair rnds (uneven and even rnd). For example, first repeat: Repeat Rnds 1 and 2, two times—4 rnds in all. Even rnds are worked in the same color that the uneven row they follow. Color changes occur only on uneven rows.

When pattern is complete, BO loosely with CC2: K1, *k1, insert left needle into the 2 sts on right needle from the back to the front and k2tog* until all the sts are worked.

Finishing

Fold the waistband in two along the purl st line and sew down on the inside. Leave a little opening, draw the elastic band through, sew both ends together, and close the opening. Sew a few sts on both sides of the skirt; secure elastic together with knit fabric to avoid it rolling up. Darn in the ends but don't cut them off yet. Hand wash in lukewarm water, lay flat to dry. Pull out the scallops and pin. When dry, remove pins and cut off ends.

KEY	
□	k
ⓞ	yo
−	p
╱	k2tog
╲	ssk
▨	MC, 2 strands
▨	CC1, 2 strands
▨	CC2, 2 strands
▨	CC3, 2 strands
▨	CC4, 2 strands
□	CC5, 2 strands
▨	1 strand CC1, 1 strand CC5
▨	1 strand CC5, 1 strand CC4
▨	1 strand CC4, 1 strand CC3
▨	1 strand CC3, 1 strand MC

KLUKKA SKIRT CHART

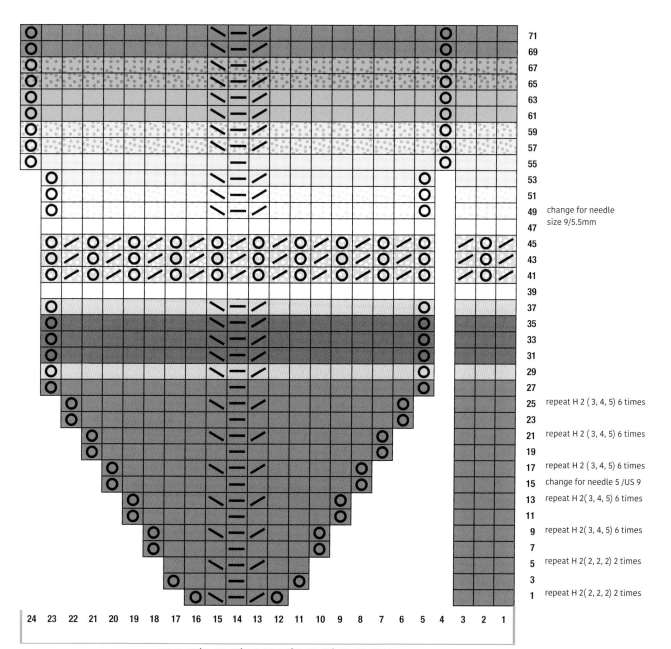

71
69
67
65
63
61
59
57
55
53
51
49   change for needle
47   size 9/5.5mm
45
43
41
39
37
35
33
31
29
27
25   repeat H 2 (3, 4, 5) 6 times
23
21   repeat H 2 (3, 4, 5) 6 times
19
17   repeat H 2 (3, 4, 5) 6 times
15   change for needle 5 /US 9
13   repeat H 2(3, 4, 5) 6 times
11
9   repeat H 2(3, 4, 5) 6 times
7
5   repeat H 2(2, 2, 2) 2 times
3
1   repeat H 2(2, 2, 2) 2 times

24   23   22   21   20   19   18   17   16   15   14   13   12   11   10   9   8   7   6   5   4   3   2   1

repeat 8, 9, 10(11, 12, 13) 14, 15, 16(17, 18, 19) 20, 21, 22 times

Only uneven rnds are charted. Even rnds are always k. Color changes occur on uneven rnds.
When uneven row is indicated as repeated, the following even row is repeated as well.

ABBREVIATIONS

beg	begin, beginning, begins
BO	bind off
CC	contrast color
cm	centimeter(s)
cn	cable needle
CO	cast on
cont	continue, continuing
dec(s)	decrease, decreasing, decreases
dpn	double-pointed needle(s)
EOR	end of round (row)
est	establish, established
inc(s)	increase(s), increasing
k	knit
k1f&b	knit into front then back of same st (increase)
k1-tbl	knit 1 st through back loop
k2tog	knit 2 sts together (decrease)
kwise	knitwise (as if to knit)
LH	left-hand
MC	main color
mm	millimeter(s)
M1	make 1 (increase)
M1k	make 1 knitwise
M1p	make 1 purlwise
pat(s)	pattern(s)
p	purl
p1f&b	purl into front then back of same st (increase)
p1-tbl	purl 1 st through back loop
P2sso	pass the 2 slipped sts over
p2tog	purl 2 sts together (decrease)
pm	place marker
pwise	purlwise (as if to purl)

rem	remain(s), remaining
rep(s)	repeat(s), repeated, repeating
revsc	reverse single crochet (crab st)
rnd(s)	round(s)
RH	right-hand
RS	right side (of work)
sc	single crochet
sk2p	slip 1 knitwise, k2tog, pass slipped st over
sl	slip, slipped, slipping
ssk	[slip 1 st knitwise] twice from left needle to right needle, insert left needle tip into fronts of both slipped sts, knit both sts together from this position (decrease)
ssp	[slip 1 st knitwise] twice from left needle to right needle, return both sts to left needle and purl both together through back loops
st(s)	stitch(es)
St st	stockinette stitch
tbl	through back loop
tog	together
w&t	wrap next stitch then turn work (often used in short rows)
WS	wrong side (of work)
wyib	with yarn in back
wyif	with yarn in front
yo	yarn over
*	repeat instructions from *
( )	alternate measurements and/or instructions
[ ]	instructions to be worked as a group a specified number of times

SPECIAL TECHNIQUES

Crochet Picot Cast-On

Step 1:
First Cast-On Stitch: Make s slipknot on the crochet hook. Hold the needle in the left hand and the crochet hook in the right hand. with the yarn under the needle, wrap the yarn under the needle and clockwise around the crochet hook as shown. Pull the yarn through the slipknot.

Step 2:
2nd (and Following) Cast-On Stitches: Bring the yarn back under the needle, wrap the yarn as before and pull it through the loop on the hook.

Step 3:
Make the Picot Loop: With crochet hook, make 3 "freestanding" chain sts.

Step 4:
Close the Picot Loop: Single crochet through the bottom of the last cast-on st on the needle (i.e., the one that was made in Step 2).

Step 5:
Repeat a pattern of cast on 3 sts (as in Step 2) and chain 3 sts and secure (as in Steps 3 and 4) until you have cast on 1 st short of the desired total number of sts.

Step 6:
Final Stitch: For the last st, bring yarn in back; slip the loop from the crochet hook onto the needle as shown.

Marking, Sewing, and Cutting a Steek

Step 1: Measure the diameter of the sleeve at the turning ridge before the facing. Mark the armhole depth on the body based on this measurement. Use a contrasting piece of cotton yarn to baste a line between the two center underarm stitches from the side marker (still on the needle) to the bottom of the armhole; make sure to clearly mark the bottom of the armhole. This basting yarn will be your cutting line.

Marking Armhole

Cutting Armhole

Step 2: Thread the sewing machine with a contrasting thread and set the machine to small stitches. Place the knitting under the machine foot and begin to sew, slowly moving the basted armhole forward; do not allow the fabric to pucker. Stitch on top of the knitted stitches *adjacent to* the basting yarn, going from the shoulder to the bottom of the armhole; turn, sew across bottom stitches of the armhole, then sew back up on the top of the knitted stitches *adjacent to* the other side of the basting thread. You should have a long, narrow "U" machine-stitched around the basting yarn. Try to avoid sewing in the "ditch," or over the bars between the stitches, since this does not catch enough of the fiber for a strong steek.

NOTE: Some knitters prefer to sew the shoulder seam together at this point to prepare the garment for sewing in the sleeves. This will minimize any extra handling of the garment once the sleeve opening is cut. The raw stitches will be exposed for a shorter time than if the shoulder seam is joined after the cutting.

Step 3: Cut along the basting yarn to open up the armhole. Sew the sleeve into place 1–2 stitches from the cut edge on each side, attaching the sleeve along the first row of the facing.

Three-Needle Bind-Off

With RS's together and needles parallel, using a third needle, knit together a stitch from the front needle and a stitch from the back. *Knit together a stitch from the front and back needles and slip the first stitch over the second stitch to bind off. Repeat from * across, then fasten off last stitch.

Knitting from Left to Right

If you want to knit entrelac, it is helpful to learn how to knit from left to right (KLR). KLR is worked when you would normally turn the work and purl back. With the use of this technique, you can knit "backward" without turning the work; this eliminates the need to turn the fabric back and forth on 6 stitches. Many knitters have found this technique helpful when making bobbles or working the heel of a sock. Learning how to KLR will make entrelac knitting much more enjoyable.

Instructions

To knit a practice swatch in stockinette stitch using this technique:

Cast on 20 sts.

Row 1: Knit.

Row 2 (WB): *Without turning,* work back (WB) using the KLR technique.

Row 3: Without turning, knit.

It may seem awkward at first, but a few minutes of trying this out will make the entrelac knitting experience more rewarding and less frustrating.

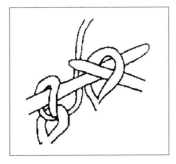

Step 1:

With LH needle, go through the *back* of the first st on RH needle.

Step 2:

Wrap yarn *over* the LH needle counterclockwise.

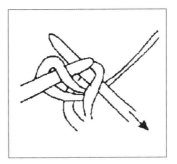

Step 3:

Draw newly formed st through old sts and slide RH needle out of old st, leaving new st on LH needle.

Crochet Cast-On (use as Provisional Cast-On)

With waste yarn make a slip stitch and place it on a crochet hook. Put the waste yarn behind the knitting needle and hook it with the crochet hook. Use the hook to pull a new loop through the loop already on the hook. Repeat these two steps until there are enough stitches on the needle. Enlarge the last loop on the crochet hook until it is about 4"/10cm long, then cut the yarn at the top of the loop and pull out the yarn attached to the ball, being careful not to pull the remaining tail, which will be removed later.

Kitchener Stitch

Place the stitches that are to be joined on two needles with needle points facing to the right. Hold needles parallel, with wrong sides together. Thread a tapestry needle with your yarn.

1. Front needle: slip the first st as if to k off the needle and go into next st on front needle as if to p and leave it on the needle, pull through both sts.

2. Back needle: slip the first st as if to p off the needle and go into next st on back needle as if to k and leave it on the needle, pull through both sts.

Repeat steps 1 and 2 for all sts on both needles. Remember to keep the working yarn beneath the needles when going from needle to needle.

Fulling (or felting)

Fulling is the process of shrinking an already-formed fabric by applying moisture, heat, and agitation. For knitted objects, this process is best done in a washing machine set on the hot, heavy-duty, ultra-clean cycle. Add ¼ cup fabric softener and 1 tablespoon vinegar to help the fiber scales open, then close, locking them together. Putting a pair of jeans or a tennis ball into the machine will help increase the agitation. For best results, run the item through the wash cycle only, checking the progress periodically. Allowing the object to go through the spin cycle may put creases in the fabric that can be hard to remove later. Some yarns and colors will need to go through the wash cycle twice or more. When the object has reached the desired size, remove from the machine, rinse in lukewarm water, shape as necessary, and allow to dry thoroughly.

Applied I-cord

With double-pointed needles, CO 3 stitches in MC.

K2, k2tog-tbl (attaching MC I-cord to edge st from pick-up), repeat along edge to end, k3tog.

Technique 1A: Afterthought Thumb

An afterthought hole can be useful for making a peasant-style thumb or an afterthought sock heel.

To Mark the Hole:

Knit the stitches indicated with contrasting scrap yarn.

Place stitches back on left needle.

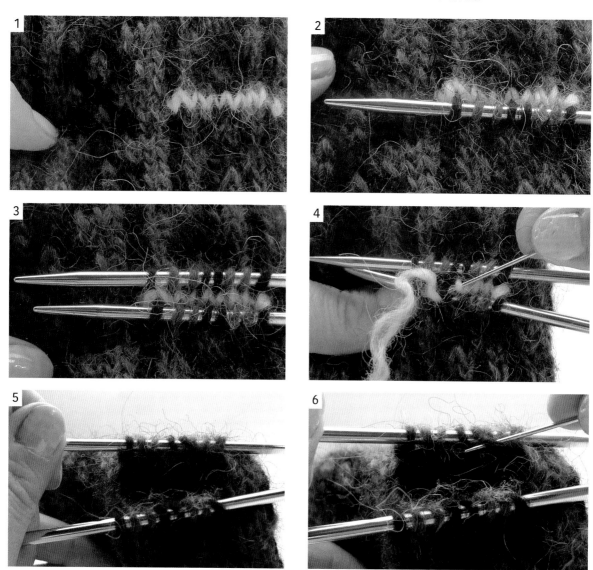

Knit them again in pattern motif, k to EOR (1).

Pick up stitches around the hole by inserting needle under the right leg of each stitch.

under (2)

above (3)

Remove scrap yarn using a threading needle, for example (4). Stitches are on needle ready to knit (5).

When knitting a stranded motif, some picked up stitches may look strange (6) because they are in fact both the stitch and the float, but once knitted, they will be just fine.

Closing the Gaps

The afterthought hole leaves two gaps on each side of the hole that need to be closed. They can be closed afterward by sewing. The gaps can also be closed by picking up a stitch in the gap; this will make an extra stitch, often desirable for a three-dimensional thumb, which can be suppressed by knitting 2 stitches together in the next round. This may still leave tiny holes that can be closed afterward by sewing.

Technique 1B: Double-Lifted Decrease

A double-lifted decrease can also be worked to close the gap. This method will add an extra st but leave no holes at all (6).

When coming to the hole, with the tip of right needle, lift the stitch on left needle (1) from the row under onto left needle (2).

With the tip of right needle, lift the stitch on same needle (3) from 2 rows under onto left needle (4) (you can also lift it with the tip of left needle and correct the mount of this second stitch).

Knit the two stitches together (5).

YARN WEIGHT SYSTEM

Categories of yarn, gauge ranges, and recommended
needle and hook sizes

Yarn Weight Symbol & Category Names	0 Lace	1 Super Fine	2 Fine	3 Light	4 Medium	5 Bulky	6 Super Bulky
Type of Yarns in Category	Fingering, 10 count Crochet Thread	Sock, Fingering, Baby	Sport, Baby	DK, Light Worsted	Worsted, Afghan, Aran	Chunky, Craft, Rug	Bulky, Roving
Knit Gauge Range* in Stockinette Stitch to 4 inches	33–40** sts	27–32 sts	23–26 sts	21–24 sts	16–20 sts	12–15 sts	6–11 sts
Recommended Needle in Metric Size Range	1.5–2.25 mm	2.25–3.25 mm	3.25–3.75 mm	3.75–4.5 mm	4.5–5.5 mm	5.5–8 mm	8mm and larger
Recommended Needle U.S. Size Range	000 to 1	1 to 3	3 to 5	5 to 7	7 to 9	9 to 11	11 and larger
Crochet Gauge* Ranges in Signle Crochet to 4 inch	32–42 double crochets**	21–31 sts	16–20 sts	12–17 sts	11–14 sts	8–11 sts	5–9 sts
Recommended Hook in Metric Size Range	Steel*** 1.6–1.4mm Regular hook 2.25mm	2.25–3.5 mm	3.5–4.5 mm	4.5–5.5 mm	5.5–6.5 mm	6.5–9 mm	9mm and larger
Recommended Hook U.S. Size Range	Steel*** 6, 7, 8 Regular hook B–1	B–1 to E–4	E–4 to 7	7 to I–9	I–9 to K–10 ½	K–10 ½ to M–13	M–13 and larger

* GUIDELINES ONLY: The above reflect the most commonly used gauges and needle or hook sizes for specific yarn categories.

** Lace weight yarns are usually knitted or crocheted on larger needles and hooks to create lacy, openwork patterns. Accordingly, a gauge range is difficult to determine. Always follow the gauge stated in your pattern.

*** Steel crochet hooks are sized differently from regular hooks—the higher the number, the smaller the hook, which is reverse of regular hook sizing.

This Standards & Guidelines booklet is available at: YarnStandards.com.

YARN SOURCES

Websites for the yarns used in the projects in this book are below. If you would like an alternate option for any yarn, or if a yarn has been discontinued, you can go to www.yarnsub.com to find options for substitution.

Blackberry Ridge Woolen Mill
www.blackberry-ridge.com

Cascade Yarns
www.cascadeyarns.com

Louet North America
www.louet.com

Ewetopia Fiber Shop
www.ewetopiafibershop.com

Ístex
www.istex.is

Love Story by Hélène Magnússon
www.icelandicknitter.com

Knit Picks
www.knitpicks.com

Misti International
www.mistialpaca.com

Raumagarn
www.theyarnguys.com

INDEX